D1193894

THE SELECTED POEMS OF
JOHN MALCOLM BRINNIN

Books by John Malcolm Brinnin

Poems

THE GARDEN IS POLITICAL
THE LINCOLN LYRICS
NO ARCH, NO TRIUMPH
THE SORROWS OF COLD STONE
THE SELECTED POEMS OF JOHN MALCOLM BRINNIN

Biography

DYLAN THOMAS IN AMERICA
THE THIRD ROSE: GERTRUDE STEIN AND HER WORLD

Criticism

EMILY DICKINSON, *a selection of poems*
CASEBOOK ON DYLAN THOMAS, *a collection of essays*
WILLIAM CARLOS WILLIAMS, *a critical study*

Anthologies

MODERN POETRY: AMERICAN AND BRITISH
(*with Kimon Friar*)

THE MODERN POETS: AN AMERICAN-BRITISH ANTHOLOGY
(*with Bill Read*)

For children

ARTHUR, THE DOLPHIN WHO DIDN'T SEE VENICE

THE
SELECTED
POEMS
OF
JOHN
MALCOLM
BRINNIN

An Atlantic Monthly Press Book

LITTLE, BROWN AND COMPANY · BOSTON · TORONTO

LIBRARY OF CONGRESS CATALOG CARD NO. 63–13976

FIRST EDITION

Certain of these poems appeared originally in *Accent, Chimera, Contempo-
rary Poetry, Harper's, Harper's Bazaar, Harvard Advocate, Kenyon Review,
Mademoiselle, New Directions Annual, New Republic, New World Writing,
Origenes* (Havana), *Poetry: A Magazine of Verse, Quarterly Review of
Literature, Sewanee Review, Southern Review, Tiger's Eye, Trinity Review,
Vice Versa, Virginia Quarterly Review,* and in the volumes *The Garden Is
Political* (Macmillan), *No Arch, No Triumph* (Knopf) and *The Sorrows of
Cold Stone* (Dodd, Mead). The following poems originally appeared in
The New Yorker: "American Plan," "A Thin Façade for Edith Sitwell,"
"Cape Ann: A View," "Friday Afternoon," "Glorious Victory of the Sloop
Maria," "Heavy Heavy Heavy," "Hotel Paradiso e Commerciale," "Ich
Am of Irlaunde," "Love in Particular," "News from the Islands," "Song
for Strangers in Wales," "Song from the Outer Office," "Return of the
Natives: Pier 90," "The Ascension: 1925," "The Giant Turtle Grants an
Interview," "Virginia City, Nev."

ATLANTIC–LITTLE, BROWN BOOKS
ARE PUBLISHED BY
LITTLE, BROWN AND COMPANY
IN ASSOCIATION WITH
THE ATLANTIC MONTHLY PRESS

*Published simultaneously in Canada
by Little, Brown & Company (Canada) Limited*

PRINTED IN THE UNITED STATES OF AMERICA

for

Jack Thompson

— the shores of Grosse Pointe

— the towers of Trebizond

CONTENTS

III

IV

V

VI

VII

VIII

*Translations from the Poetry of
Jorge Carrera Andrade*

IX

X

I

OBSERVATORY HILL

Surprised in this blue poise of evening,
I watch the white observatory dome that turns
And stops, and hugely opening,
Submits a complex eye
To the indifference of eternity
Like some astonished chick
Cracking a shell to try its excellence.
Involved with natural law,
I feel that utter breakage in my hands
And, in a loud light, see
My shores and settled frontiers struck from view.
As the new chick on fragments settles back,
The telescope retires to its womb,
I bunch my coat and, chilly, cut for home.

Boxed at the nervy center of a house,
I watched a spectacle of stars
Like inward microbes fastened to my heart,
And knew the windows false,
And met that evil order looking straight.
Let Whitman go, and all the rest
Who turned their broad glad faces on the West;
Since all deliberate innocence must fail,
Call back the heart, the naïve heart, and tell —

[3]

Yes, even your blind agony will do —
How those of single vision are brought down:
The mad, in furs, dead at the coldest poles,
The aviators choked in high inhuman air,
All hunters of a fable of white whales
Who, planting their acquisitive eyes
On one horizon opposite death,
Must, somewhere in that self-destroying chase,
Burn to the purposive bones of faith;
Giving madness its fragment of valor
Until, wrapped in a bravery of mistakes,
They find their graves in learned paradox.

From those circumferences returned,
I fixed the impartial lens and telescopic eye
Dead center down and learned
Beethoven's triumph in his muffled room,
Saw Vincent's bleeding ear in a golden frame,
Walked blind with Joyce, while through the sensual gloom,
Alternatively riding and at bay,
The music of heroic heresy
Sang like an underwater bell
Through every hammered syllable.
I knew forever then the last frontier
Not to be reached by coasting over land
Toward an Atlantic or Pacific strand
But, like the perishable isle of coral drowned,
In constricted channel found
Lonely and not for long; for the single traveler
Who greets it with penultimate despair
Frontier becomes exit and entrance there.
O mineral metaphor
Within whose strict and diamond eye

My sight is fractured and set free,
In whose expansive process shine
The lifted tentacle, the dreaming head
And Wednesday's dead,
Surrendered down, contracted to your tragedy,
I read the stars and find their eyes on mine.
Let all brave bones go clattering into fable;
I must make my bed, I must set my table.

OEDIPUS: HIS CRADLE SONG

WHO is my shepherd, that I shall not want?
Who with earth-roughened hands
Will loose the spike that joins my anklebones,
And bear me home, and have me in his house?

I seek a father who most need a son,
Yet have no voice to call
One or the other, nor wind nor oracle
To publish me, where I am meant to die.

Who is my uncle, that shall intervene,
Assist the turning wheel
That like the running towers of the sun
Will smash my king's house and my cockleshell?

Who is my mother, that shall make my bed?
Who with gold-beaten rings
Shall quicken me, that I beget my son
Where my cold father with his lust lay down?

Who is one blind, that has already seen
Blood where it shall fall soon?
He knows my ways and how I rule this ground.
In his perpetual light I would be found.

The day is in the sea, the night grows cold.
Is the event long past?
The suckling beast knows where I lie alone.
I seek a father who most need a son.

[6]

FÊTES, FATES

O NOT to bless my soul
Come kinsmen wrist, thigh, lip and all their creatures,
Guests of my board and bed,
Companions of intolerable pleasure,
Whiplashing tongue, arched eyebrow, swiveled head
Who, by blood's stream and vessel,
Make picnic of my will,
Eating its music with an insect measure,
Unraveling its laws
Piecemeal, until, in the disgrace of nature,
Whim is my wantonness
And wit's my jack-of-all.

Their host and cage long since,
I haunt the drunken table where they take
The welcome of my house,
And cannot shade my eyes nor turn my back
When their unruly fragments kiss and toss
Sense to its blunted sense,
Love on its dear love's clowns.
To mend me, mind me, bind me where I break —
Heart's blood, mind's rift of light —
Is all my will; all, all, my lack:
Those meshings make my fate,
Those hungers call my dance.

[7]

Goodnight, when the door swings
And the great lock's shuttle tooth comes down
On darkness and hail fellow,
Goodnight, my smile, insatiate eye, bald frown,
Goodnight. In colder carnivals we'll follow
Our one pleasaunce among
A quietude, ere long,
That will our disparateness so bundle down
In earthen intimacy,
My ways and will and yours will move as one,
When guest by host shall lie
Lengthwise, and right by wrong.

LOVE IN PARTICULAR

WHEN the orchard that clings to the terrace is boxed for
        the winter
And birds take the sun deck and the first hieroglyph of snow
Sprawls on the darkening side street under crawling cars,
        There is much to be reconsidered
        About the nature of this place;
        Because of all doomed capitals
        Certainly none was less
        Love's climate or to its light more false.

In the encroaching blue of its twilight, the exciting
Approach of still another enormous evening, how many
Desolate figures watch the first lights of Radio City
        Burn for a little while —
        As those who in great harbors,
        Framed in a thousand portholes,
        Attend the huge maneuverings of liners
        And the infinitesimal farewells?

Each to his own fake fireplace, each to his hobby
Of glass elephants that trumpet in duplicate herds
Across twenty square inches of table-top mirror,

While the modest leaf of love
Fumes like a steaming orchid
In the center of the room,
Costly, rootless, and naked,
And disappears like flame.

Ah, the swift matings and undernourished affections,
The pledge of troth as tidy as a business deal
Of unexpected advancement with a comfortable equity;
In their profitless commerce at midnight,
Pulverous shadows strive
To gain their random image,
While bartenders give them nerve
And the bankers give homage.

To admit that this is not an accident but an achievement
Is but to marry St. Patrick's to the Onyx Club
With dancing afterwards and mingling of the guests,
For in the sacrifice of appetite,
The angel of love hangs in the sky
Like a corpse of warning.
Many murders are in his eye
Every blessed morning.

The lights and lives that stratify these avenues
Shine at the frayed nerve ends of a prodigious hunger
Not to be answered by a million appetites
For love without identity
Or burned to exhaustion in a night
Of gaiety and anger;
For the anarchies of appetite
Are not the feasts of hunger.

Leave it, then, to an impromptu drift of snow,
Some falling, final, graciousness of snow
That brings its trophies and mistakes to burial;
       If to begin again
       Means other faces, other ambitions,
       Love is as long as time
       And as full of notions.
       Let the day perish, let the day come.

THE MARGINAL DARK

Rain, like a traveler, walks on the night.
Skyscrapers make their cubist gestures where
The reach of man outruns his mortal height;
The intermittent multitudes are here,
Grouped by the rain in doorways, stopped in flight
Between commercial houses and the night.

I go among them since I must; transformed
Upon the sidewalks, I assume their eyes
And go misshapen with them to their charmed
Arenas, their contrived realities
Of cinema and song; we leave unharmed
Though death is neighbor with his face transformed.

Assembled underground, we wait for trains
That move through darkness like the track of time;
We, cripples, negatives of promise, lean
Our crutch of bones upon a scribbled beam;
While the loud year beats impartially, like rain
On eloquent marble, we await our trains.

Night of this night, there is a prayer in me
Who read my destination in their love.
May this black cancer and this leprosy
The sovereign brand of our conjunction prove.
This is my world among the beasts who see;
In them I endure the night, and they in me.

JOHN THE BAPTIST

WITH gulls for escort and with grace
Of spring come down to Battery Park and more,
John the Baptist bore
His holy folio into that town;
His lion's eyes that shone
With deep Judean eminence were less
Than certain in that place,
And his tawny face was lit
Wondrously with doubt. *Am I, in truth, too late?*
He said, watching the gulls and the towers,
The streets and the ominous signs on the shores.

A brilliant wilderness, he thought,
Turning for photographs his large sad eyes,
Pronouncing for the press
His sacerdotal words upon the deck;
When, scissoring at his back,
Some dexterous fanatic lunged to cut
A relic from his coat,
And a momentary gull
Submerged its eyes into the sea to pull
A dripping morsel from the deep. O John,
Those warning angels in the morning sun!

*   *   *

All this was several years ago.
You've had it in the print how Herod
Immortally errored;
And that dark dancer from the Paradise Roof,
How she accounted life
No more than lustful acclamation. O,
It was grief to see him go
Unchampioned. For when
His prophet's head, lolling and dead, had been
On some commercial platter deftly placed,
What vistas and what news were sacrificed!

Yet still the visionaries trip
Through golden gates, and up the dark north rivers;
Sweet simpletons, they never
Know what heresies parade our sun's
Unscrupulous pavilions;
Within their monumental hearts they keep
The naïveté of sheep,
Welcoming, shout to see
Musicians moving and the kingly play;
And when the fatal girls come dancing out,
Their ardor is most ruinously bought.

AT THE MUSEUM

COLLECTORS are abroad, the nets are spread.
The clipped wing and the fluted cameo
Submit their shapes to mummy-case and shelf;
Where antiquated triplanes hang like clowns
And dinosaurs await the floods of dusk,
Time like a document lies under glass.

Outside, the living beat upon the doors
Impatient to be catalogued and done;
The buses pass the impotent stone lions,
While crowds, in shapes of crocodile or lamb,
Rehearse the Roman holiday again,
Through festivals of mourning bear their dead.

On stilted legs, the hooded cameras
Pursue them to their rooms — the lonesome Self
Whose only memories are photographs:
"With Annabelle at Palisades. Cute kid,"
Or, on some childhood strand, the Family
Absurdly happy in their bathing suits.

Collectors are abroad, the nets are spread,
And I would ask of them a single prize:
By rummaging the careless earth to find
Not wings, nor wheels, nor kettles in a tomb,
But one unwritten scroll of flesh that proves
That men are gods, the blessed and the unblessed.

THE WIND IS ILL

All's ill and will be so
Until what will not wed is brought to bed
Charged with a savior's brief
For coupling conscience with black flesh and blood;
Until the arch supports its crushing roof,
And eggs in nests of snow
Drown the long undertow
With clattering allelulias from the shell,
All's well so charily
The tongues of iron bells will fail to tell
A wiser homily than verily,
Say lack, say touch and go.

All hail wind-cocks that shift
The livelong architecture of the mind
From leaf-pocked flesh to stone;
Where blunt-nosed marbles, eaten by the wind,
Drift grain by grain to cover Babylon,
East comes soft, west comes swift,
Until, of all that's left,
Scrolls of flesh and hammered tablets tell
All ails so bitterly
The dove with news is buried where it fell,
And banished utterly
The little dog that laughed.

All hell pursues the pair
Who first touched fruits of flesh to find them sweet
But sadly separate;
The hunt is hot and what is chaste is caught,
Stripped of its leaf and tangled in a sheet
While the bored glories sit
Before and after it,
Clocking the chores of ecstasy untouched.
Ah, well, the wind is ill,
And if such sails as loom are seldom beached,
Farewell's the most of hail,
Here, there, and everywhere.

TO THE PRIEST IN THE WINDOW SEAT

FATHER, we have left the ground
You smudged my forehead with one darker Wednesday,
    And now the Te Deum Laudamus sound
Of four cowled Pratt and Whitney engines sends my

    Thoughts toward years when, in your charge,
I felt the tendrils of my soul grown large

    Beyond the husbandry I could command,
And heard you, muffled in a cloth,
Forgive my sins with a half-lifted hand,
And teach me how elastic was our faith.

    Never did I think we'd meet
With both feet in the air nor, parted, share —
    Two thirds of trinity — a triple seat,
Nor guess that, in this Appalachian air,

    The same assumption would not hold
For both of us. And yet, as if foretold

    In that sly preference of opposites
For what will undermine them, we exchange
A journey's pleasantries of smiles and lights
And, parallel, refuse to find them strange.

If I, like that black angel, Joyce,
Have for the millionth time gone forth to meet
    Reality, to forge in my soul not grace
But this world's unborn conscience, is not fate
    The heresy on which we part?
What I have mind for, you can have no heart.
    Still, by this dedicated waywardness,
I feel strangely at one with you,
A prodigal whose silence is, like yours,
Uplifted by the grandeur of the view.

    Two souls in mortal flight, we take
Sustaining morsels from a pillowed tray
    And, on heaven's business and the world's, sit back
To think on whence we came and where we go.
    Midwestern sunlight blinds us now,
And while we cannot see our wings, we know,
    By a long-traveled faith, they are still there.
I shall miss you, Father, and may want your pity,
When you go on toward higher ground somewhere,
And I get off, as planned, in Kansas City.

BEFORE THERE WAS NO REASON
IN THE WORLD

BEFORE there was no reason in the world
As now there is
I was the bough bent easy by a bird
I was the vague blue-grazing flock
The sleeping and invisible

Before there was no reason in the world
As now there is
The course of waters was my only course
My repetitions oceans' sough and swell
My seasons pleasurable

Before there was no reason in the world
As now there is
To measure time from sleep I rose to sleep
To measure space I pastured on surprise
O meadows of resemblances

Before there was no reason in the world
As now there is
I was the grove on whose mosaic floors
The seeds of otherwise were spent
My gods had many arms

I was the Caesar of unmarshaled grass
Faustus in the branches
My first ambitions were my sorrows long
Before there was no reason in the world
As now there is

[20]

II

NOT FAR FROM ARARAT

So in their term elect did man and beast
Sleep forty nights under bare rib and rafter,
And eastward float as the dead sun went west;
In the gay dreams none would remember after,
Flesh on cold flesh that never said a word
Endured the dark that would not be endured;
And lion by gazelle was scoured to bone.
How every mad start and solo of the Lord
(He sang from a bush! Came gushing from a stone!)
Seemed but the weather and that time of year
And nothing in particular.
So did they in the great drift of things sail on,
Their hopes obeying heaven's, their hearts face down.
And when the rain drummed murmurs on their roof,
They put a soft pigeon out for proof.
If it were all true, and they would be reclaimed,
If at the end the vast beginning seemed
Already long accounted for;
If, unabashed, one of the daughters wore,
About her swelling waist
And hip, the forepaw of a nameless beast,
At last, by the endurance of a dove,
Things as they were were made believable.
On that good morning when they set their table,
The reek of meat rose with their choirs of love.

THE GEORGIAN HOUSE

THE great house flames from out its blinded eyes
And every cracked and sabotaged beam falls
Across the darkening bodies; little mice
Flee fanwise, and a burning parrot calls
For sweetmeats, sweetmeats in his gilded room.

That Georgian mansion, whose surrendered gloom
And neo-classic pillars charmed a race
Of fathers, settles, guilty, to its doom
Ablaze with contradictions and disease.
Only the galleried ancestor, whose cold

Accumulating eye maintains its walled
Intransigence, looks on, while careful flames,
Reception hall to scullery, attic to vault,
Explore the baroque order of decay.
Collapsing like a draughty argument,

That world regime submits its eminent
Remains to time; the old lie with the young.
As mystery burns in its own evidence,
Obedient, the bones sing: Right or wrong,
I was my prodigal father's faithful son.

So have the torches of the mind undone
A mindless monument; and where the scarred
Allotments of its history wait the sun
And builders, nothing comes; no thing apart,
Whose memory is human, or whose heart.

[24]

CADILLAC SQUARE: 1933

WHOEVER know a city, know this square:
The loud and quaking air
That breaks on brick or scales the sun-choked glass,
The travelers who pass
One minute of one day and nevermore,
The neo-Grecian door
Poised like the needle's eye, open and shut
For the mythical feet
Of some squat nobleman of fields and mines,
Industrial scenes,
Or eggshell yachts afloat in summer water,
The pink expensive daughter
With a flair for shady friends and maybe Bach,
The colonnaded house and the Chinese cook.

In early spring this heartlike acre shines:
Canyoned streets, carlines
Flow with violence of union, men
Learn faith in fathers then;
The butcher from the suburb and the clerk
Hear the organizers speak
The echoing language of the pioneer,
And in that press they cheer
With such a swirling and reproachless voice
The city swims in noise;

Those sooty faces and grime-sculptured hands
Live where the river bends,
They own the rotted gardens made to green
Where but the fossils of machines have lain.

All interweaves among the changing years:
Progress is in arrears
Until some chanticleering message raids
The disparate multitudes,
Or the bark of some command, made sharp with hate,
Sends Property's gunmen out.
Poised in that infinity of death
Or life, or barely both,
The human balance sways; away, away,
The bleak night and the day,
The bankers couched in limousines, the poor
Jackknifed against a door,
The bankers conscious of defeat, the poor
Jackknifed, oblivious, against a door.

SPENDING his whole experience of space
With handsome fallacy, the burning boy
Swan-dives toward his marine metropolis
And in the plumage of blue water-smoke
Makes boiling colors all his languages.

How laughable the hiss of this sea-death:
The fine blond energy so spluttered out,
Its arc no matter more than a tossed match
Or a comet swallowed over conversation.
How thin the sheetings of this marriage-bed.

Since lack and love sing only at their crisis,
His music falls forwards and afterwards;
See how the diver is himself dissolved
Where irises on the dilating pool
Drop one free-floating feather for a child!

Is talk of weddings, then, but talk of death,
And every day but where he dies again?
His crystal city a submergèd hope,
Half water-light, half memory? The sea
Drags under what it cannot free.

So in a wink a flying hand farewells
A decade's love or love for twenty minutes
With the same flame. How now these whispering shells
And rocking skulls forever souvenir
The first and ultimate waters of it all.

THE LATE SUMMER

To say, Change Cometh, set the old scene straight,
Mark off long summer in a frame of kites
Pegging the four blue corners of the wind;
So turns my purpose backward, chilled with leaves.

Like voyagers who, slow to lose the weave
Of seas beneath them, waver on the shore,
So am I beached upon this running strand
While underwater all Manhattan tolls.

Now shall I range the sands half-mad,
And speak in parables to the swift sun?
My hands are curious, when driftwood comes,
Testing a branch, or tracing lettering.

If, in the manner of the books, some sail
Comes riding over all that scattered loss,
May I rejoice for piracy and thieves,
Beat on a drum, scrimmage for preference?

Go down, my summertime, with every kite
That, like a roving anchor, drags my heart;
Come, summer like a masterpiece, come, sky,
Demand to be remembered, framed and false.

BEING apprised of day,
Of night's licentious torch
And all earth's sea-wracked shores,
Metropolis and plain;
Having but learned to scan
Idea and issue, and to march
The dialectic way,

With the tragedian
I understand, and bow,
Since all my heroes seem
As false as pitiful;
Hope was their principle,
Affirmed to spite the public blow
Like Punch, a child's comedian.

Twisting with antic all
The grieved and crippled past,
They sowed an optimistic seed,
Implanting emeralds where
The realer pebbles were,
Devising chances for the least,
A slipper at a ball.

[29]

None dared to stop,
The unreal or the real,
Romantic as our own
Who would transcend the slum,
Self-exiled to become
Gay Faustus at the wheel
Outstepping all the cops.

Abnormally we dream
And all our colors are
Half-stained by death, who come
From adolescence scored,
Already, on the marksman's board;
What embryos we are
We hurry to become.

So the mind strings out its kites
Zigzag across the plains;
Then, like a furious child,
Perverse with dreams, intent,
Mortal predicament
Comes slowly to the sense;
Touched with that zero, lights

Of intellect shine thin;
When late, with blunted eyes
We cruelly see, the minds
Of all are frozen still
As grounded kites, until,
Across our shrapnel-printed skies,
The naïve heart floats in.

HEROES

WHERE are the heroes promised in the books,
Coming with dignity, riding the crowds,
Shaking the air with plumed, commanding looks?

They are not here. Only the clowns are proud,
Beneath the gargoyled characters they wear,
To sing their solo emptiness aloud.

And as the sun draws sunflowers to stare
With large bald eyes into the summer's flame,
So turn our multitudes who share

The same compelling sky, the same sweet loam;
We are those answerable to suns that spin
Hypnotic coinage in the path of fame;

Beguiled and gently cheated, we begin,
Day after day, the false admiring stare,
Drained to the root, turned watery within.

Time's pictured heroes are not anywhere,
Nor may a scrapbook claim their autographs;
All those who move with heroism here

Recount our difficult and common life;
The simple are imperial today.
A schoolyard tumbling child has had enough

Of learning tales of giants and their ways,
Since mortal families of the innocent
Deserve his imitation and his praise.

GRAVE MIND I LOVED

GRAVE mind I loved, of all who mind your grave
Or lie beside, I know that John Donne's ghost
Recants the dying falls, the skull-capped love
Deaths and quick rime that — how long since! — would **try**
Our inarticulate mortality,
Needling for dust the flesh we favored most.

Sleep sound, sweet foundling, though I'd sound your sleep;
Make what you will of metaphysic bone,
I will not mind. Until my time is up,
Take heart, my heart, if a ghost may have one,
Have done with John's thin image and have Donne.

THE FAIR OF SUMMER

Wₙₜₕ such sweet carriage even orchards melt,
Over miraculous escarpments where
Tomorrows show their treatises and halt
Upon each dawn intemperately, the fair
Of summer, pennants in the sand and gilt
Sea-creatures, plants a broad tent everywhere;
Then on its burning floor July displays
Its equinoctial merchandise.

Up mountainsides, attempting danger, boys
Will swing about and give themselves to plains,
And deep among the rocks' recess and noise
Of waterfalls and miniature terrains,
Philosophers will turn a blade of grass
Or put it in their teeth and whistle tunes;
No one expects a goddess from the rock,
Though if she came she would go, ravished, back.

O everywhere that summer comes and is
The optimism of this misery,
And everywhere that blue and thoughtless eyes
Range over cliff and drumlin lucklessly,
The shadow side of years, defeated, dies
With no wise creature thereabout to see;
They will survive a crying day's despair
Who in the dead of winter wander there.

A RIVER

A WINKLESS river of the cloistered sort
Falls in its dark habit massively
Through fields where single cattle troll their bells
With long shows of indifference, and through
The fêtes champêtres of trees so grimly bent
They might be gallows-girls betrayed by time
That held them once as gently as Watteau.

Electric in its falling, passing fair
Through towns touched up with gilt and whitewash, it
Chooses oddments of discard, songs and feathers
And the stuff of life that must keep secrets
Everlastingly: the red and ratlike curios
Of passion, knives and silks and embryos
All sailing somewhere for a little while.

The midnight drunkard pausing on the bridge
Is dumbstruck with a story in his eye
Shuttling like his memories, and must
Outface five tottering steeples to admit
That what he sees pass under him is not
Mere moonlit oil and pods of floating seed,
But altogether an astonishing swan.

The river, I mean, for all is riverine,
Goes slowly inward, as one would say of time,
So it goes, and thus proceed to gather in
The dishes of a picnic, or the bones
Of someone lost contesting with the nations,
Glad in the wisdom of his pity to serve
Though the river's knowledge, whelming, overwhelms.

HEAVY HEAVY HEAVY

WHO winds the clumsy flower-clock now, I wonder,
And opens the minaret in Waterworks Park
For bird's-eye views of captive fern and reindeer?
"Heavy heavy heavy hangs over thy head,"
The flower-clock said,
"What shall ye do to redeem it?"

Do conch shells hum in shingled bungalows
Where stop-streets subdivide eternity?
Has the crutch bloomed in St. Bartholomew's?
Crazy as preachers, running all night long,
Do empty streetcars still go off their trolleys
Trailing brimstone, tolling cling and clang?
"Heavy heavy heavy hangs over thy head,"
The trolley-car said,
"What shall ye do to redeem it?"

And there were sea gulls that far from the sea!
Once, I recall, on the soft river air,
Like a hovering Holy Ghost, one talked to me.
It was a night in spring, when ice-floes rolled
Like foggy castles in the melting rain.
"Heavy heavy heavy hangs over thy head,"
The ice-floes said,
"What shall ye do to redeem it?"

[39]

I called it my home-town, I guess, although
Constantinople seems more plausible.
I wonder if the night-shift lights still glow
Like sea-fires in a shipwrecked neighborhood.
I wonder if some still-eyed ten-year-old
Goes sidewise on the sea-floor as I did.
"Heavy heavy heavy hangs over thy head,"
The night lights said,
"What shall ye do to redeem it?"

Must time so rage behind that I still go
Face down forever toward some small event?
And does my echo know what once I knew?
"Heavy heavy heavy hangs over thy head,"
The echo, echoing, said,
"What shall ye do to redeem it?"

ROWING IN LINCOLN PARK

You are, in 1925, my father;
Straw-hatted, prim, I am your only son;
Through zebra-light fanwise on the lagoon
Our rented boat slides on the lucent calm.

And we are wistful, having come to this
First tableau of ourselves: your eyes that look
Astonished on my nine bravado years,
My conscious heart that hears the oarlocks click

And swells with facts particular to you —
How France is pink, how noon is shadowless,
How bad unruly angels tumbled from
That ivory eminence, and how they burned.

And you are vaguely undermined and plan
Surprise of pennies, some directed gesture,
Being proud and inarticulate, your mind
Dramatic and unpoised, surprised with love.

In silences hermetical as this
The lean ancestral hand returns, the voice
Of unfulfillment with its bladelike touch
Warning our scattered breath to be resolved.

And sons and fathers in their mutual eyes,
Exchange (a moment huge and volatile)
The glance of paralytics, or the news
Of master-builders on the trespassed earth.

Now I am twenty-two and you are dead,
And late in Lincoln Park the rowers cross
Unfavored in their odysseys, the lake
Not dazzling nor wide, but dark and commonplace.

LAMENT FOR THE A&P GYPSIES

HAVE that late summer as it was — September haze
Poked through by goldenrod, exhausted ferns
In doughboys' helmets hanging from white porches,
And through a neighborhood clipped neat as grass
The conversation of a thousand radios.
    Bequeath one evening its suburban blue,
        And nobody outdoors
    Except the sad prince, ten years old,
        Dressed in plus fours.

All afternoon he has dissected grasshoppers,
And now, to make a lantern of a Mason jar,
He scours the twilight after fireflies;
His chase might tease him up the Amazon,
But melodies from Pittsburgh call him home
    As, twig in hand, he plays a picket fence
        And, stepping on a crack,
    Learns how his mother's son must break
        His mother's back.

Ladybugs that fly away do not all fly home;
Star bright, he wishes neither may nor might
When in a lampshade bungalow he sees
An airedale waltzing with a full-grown man,
A woman sewing cherries on a hat.

Play while you may, the violins implore,
    Drink to me only, Come to the fair;
But, listing home, he knows they are
    Mere waves of air.

Let him keep promises; his lies are white
As, whistling, scared, through the antipodes,
His shadow grows by billboard and streetlight.
Bring him, at last, his lawn, his walk, his house:
On the tall stairs that lead to his own room,
    Turn him to stone; let him stand there forever —
        Safe home another day,
    Watching his father's hands tune in
        KDKA.

FRIDAY AFTERNOON

HERE comes Miss Lou Lou Vanderbilt.
She's fifty-two and got up like a bride
chalked life-size on a back-yard fence.
Her hat's as frosted as a birthday cake
and sets so straight it might be lit.
You shouldn't let her see you looking.
Miss Lou Lou's private as a bird.

It's Friday afternoon in the Bahamas.
She's going calling in the winter sun
with a white reticule that's full of calling cards
and something round and weighty — maybe money —
that makes the lacy netting sag.
Miss Lou Lou's absolute, dead white on black,
so Christian, so high-toned,
she's even better than she thinks she is.

They know it, that bad lot that hangs around
the Blue Moon Pool Room,
and so do those large girls in purple pants
who slouch in front of Queenie's Bar-B-Q.
Miss Lou Lou could be white in fact,
for all they seem to notice.
Yet you can tell they know she's there,
and that they ponder what she's thinking.

Pulling their gazes as a ship draws water,
she takes her time to pass the Good God Shoe Repair,
the Café Zanzibar,
and the Young Ladies Beautiful League,
and won't let one damned soul relax until
she's turned the corner of Columbus Lane.
The moony eyes break easy then, and mix like foam.

So long, Miss Lou Lou Vanderbilt,
don't mind if no one's home,
because you're the perfect snapshot negative
of my own Great-Aunt Alice.
In a cold town due north of here
she'd glisten, nights, in Pond's cold cream,
and Friday afternoons, in total black,
scatter her mite of grace and calling cards
through half a dozen stained-glass vestibules.

When, stork-straight, skirts in hand,
she'd sweep down past the Palais Royal Tea Rooms
where fox trots issued from a ragtime five,
she never saw a thing or heard a note,
and nobody paid her any mind.
Yet in the eyes of girl chums and war widows
you could tell by a kind of merry fear
they knew Aunt Alice had an awful lot to say
she never said by speaking.

THE ASCENSION: 1925

Step on it, said Aunt Alice, *for God's sake,*
The bloody thing is going up at four!
She crammed two broilers in a paper sack,
Harnessed the dog and pushed us out the door.
Flapping like a witch, our touring car
Ate black macadam toward Fort Frontenac
Where, trembling in her ropes, the ship of air
Rolled easy as a fifty-cent cigar.

Jesus, said Uncle Lester, *what a beaut!*
Chomping on Juicy Fruit, we eyed her close
As, nuzzling upward from her stake, she rose
In strict submission to the absolute.
We hit the highway sixty on the nose
And jettisoned our chicken bones en route.

SUNDAYS IN HALIFAX

THUNDER from the barn, and then
a scraping ess halfway around the house
tells us the sleigh is at the door.
Upright in the front seat,
my Uncle Abraham and Belle, the Boston bull,
study the windows with flint eyes.
We skitter in our furs downstairs
and, lumped like chocolates in a box,
set off for mass.

No silver shakes, no tassel flies
from the harness of our high-rumped bay;
nobody sings, or even speaks.
Our long steel runners, hissing at pedestrians
and big MacLaughlin-Buicks stalled in snow,
say clearly all we care to say.

Clanging its Irish through
the nicer music of the Presbyterians,
St. Andrew's bell rebukes our style as,
handing one another down,
we flow indoors with the black multitude
and genuflect by the fourth row.
The organ glooms; the big doors shut.

The Virgin, standing barefoot on a snake,
holds God on her right hand. A cool tear slides
from my armpit. My stockings itch.
I can't see anything. I'm four years old.
I have to go.

The church is cold, a cheerlessness
of standing up and sitting down and kneeling
on raw knees. My rosary
chinks to the floor. Aunt Alice gives me
her iced smile. "Pick it up,"
my mother whispers. My breath makes paths
down the black sleeve of her Alaskan seal.

Everywhere at once, the ushers
fish the pews with their long-handled baskets.
The air is filled deliciously
with dimes. I give mine up,
searching the nice man's face for gratitude,
and get nowhere. I sigh — What will become of us? —
wasting my breath. The candles burn,
but don't burn down. We are here to stay:
Aunt Alice, stiff with cancer,
entombed like an Egyptian in her plumes and jet;
my cousin Felix, ex-law student,
cutting meat in a straw hat;
the sleigh, its shafts like dead antennae,
hung from the rafters of the barn;
and Uncle Abraham, whose schooners used to roll
from Sable Island up to Labrador,
tied to the wheel of a round-bottomed ferry boat
that ducked across the harbor, side to side,
until a bridge made him extinct.

[49]

Like royalty, eyes neither right nor left,
we part the crowds on the church steps,
march en masse to our swan-shaped conveyance
and, whip in air, skim off like effigies.

The goal of our devotions is roast beef.
We dine together and digest alone:
my mother, dribbling a doily, hums
a Strauss waltz and rocks as she crochets;
upstairs, Aunt Alice dies her Sunday death
blacked out with migraine;
while a walrus head from Hudson Bay
ogles my Uncle Abraham, and sniffs his rum,
Felix, sawing wood to make a man of him,
spits on his hands and saws us all in two.
In the dead parlor where the ferns run wild,
I leaf an illustrated book
and get from Aberdeen halfway to Zanzibar.

IV

NEW YEAR'S EVE: 1939

WINTER and aseptic snow, the last
Expected gestures of the natural year
Entrap the hemisphere;
In chambers, and in lacquered clubs, the cries
Of celebrants release
A rich hysteria of girls, the thin
And wine-propped arms of men,
While sadness falls, a season of cold rain,
Since Prague is two months gone;
The shrill romantic protests have been made,
The ravaged called unfortunate, the victors mad.

That guilty epic and its legends weigh
Too mightily; the gay night is outfaced
From bleeding east to west;
A lover may not look but in his eyes
The wretched story blurs;
And yet, among the antique ruins, I trace
One luminous whole house
That stands invisible where it was built;
Its portals will not melt
Nor may the fierce designs of time unloose
Its pillars Samsonesque, its lonely peace.

Our years were young, our only crisis, love;
Desire with his scissors sharp went out

[53]

To find a grove, and cut
A tree of flowers for the double bed
(White lilacs at your head!)
And in the slums a hundred footsteps down
The Negro lights were gone,
The city skimmed on wet and summer streets;
When windy curtains put
A trelliswork across your ashen eyes,
Night was our island, love its enterprise.

Our partings made us figures on a frieze.
To know that frozen history and survive
The heart of stone must live
Possessed by silence while the seasons move.
Here was such reach of love
Would have commanded, in some other guise,
Treaties of strict peace,
Would have converted hangmen from their plans,
Deployed the raiding planes,
Put Christ in capitals and in the churches Marx,
Rung in an Easter for the orthodox.

You are not here; the frosty exit gives,
The year debased and cancerous unwinds,
Swims on through fading sounds
Into the clamped macabre pages of our text.
And whose small death is next?
Who names the untranslatable and good,
Drowned innocence in blood?
Who will evade the print, trick history,
Assume dark mastery?
The cold night moves through ether like a flame;
Loud music will not stay it, nor the lewdest name.

LETTER TO STATUES

THE taxi halts before a pale museum:
It is broad day — no time for stealth, as when
One late and melting evening I came
To learn the trick of vision from the stone
Immortals that brings the azure outside in.
My pulse-beat thundering out, I here return
These classic masks and garments to their own.
What marble means no man will ever learn.

In these disputed shades, I ask belief
That no form in my gallery shall move
With any dearer than imperfect life;
Since even Venus, in our days alone,
Ran with the shadows, would not come to love,
My next companion shall be flesh and bone.

THE PARTING

MAGNIFIED, your monstrous image moves:
Your multiple body weaves
Across the common pavement and the ice,
No unfamiliar space,
But singular, measured, calmly here to there,
An instant's hemisphere.

When, clothed in stone, my turning limbs unwrap:
Frozen on the step,
The body's cinema unspools and great
Archangels swim the night,
The lawns unfester and the boxwood quakes,
The wreck of midnight smokes
Under my face, while Time, a handless clock,
Roars across the dark.
In at the death, I call; you quickly turn;
A burning tower runs
Above that visionary traffic in the street.

I fall to my retreat,
The legendary sight of you undone,
Its careless grandeur gone,
Tall cities in my brain afire,
And tears, the last impatience of desire.

WAITING

WHAT reasons may the single heart employ
When, forward and impervious, it moves
Through savage times and science toward the joy
Of love's next meeting in a threatened space?
What privilege is this, whose tenure gives
One anesthetic hour of release,
While the air raid's spattered signature displays
A bitter artistry among the trees?

Thus, in our published era, sweetness lives
And keeps its reasons in a private room;
As, in the hothouse, white hibiscus proves
A gardener's thesis all the winter through,
So does this tenderness of waiting bloom
Like tropics under glass, my dear, for you.

BY THE LAKE

IN the florid part of mind, or on some card
A friend leaves, saying "Get well soon," that lake
Is painted — there faultless swans move in their weird
Processionals, unswerving under bridge
And willow, tracking silence like a wake;
Yet we, touched with that wonder, could explore
Those water-colored houses on its edge,
Walk, effortless, through every paper door.

Here, in the trailing landscape of a week,
I know that vista differently — not swans,
Not houses from a brush beguiled our walk
Since, that day, oil was drilled and planes were downed,
And I along those green immediate lawns
Might say your name with love, but lost the sound.

DISSERTATION

CIRCUIT of the night has wheeled
Our valley to a windless dawn,
And what the flushing evening held
Is satisfied and done.

Now in the cat's retreating hour,
Signs of careless human morn
Put loudness on my face, and there,
Whistling over ice, the horns

Berate me with familiar day.
Children are up, and legal loves
In every patent hostelry
And house: our day revolves

To creaking doors; someone departs
To give reality a gait,
And civic substance to reports
And statutes in the print tonight.

In this exact and countless dream,
This moment of the dawn's eclipse,
Turning to claim your eyes, I claim
The quick of morning on your lips.

Though earth should turn her colors out
And harbor dark for holiday,
Though planets atrophy the route
That swung them all but yesterday,

These were no miracles for fear.
I, too, accosted by those eyes,
Have watched a comet disappear
Into the heart's antipodes.

All ways toward dignity were lost
Did not the spooling sunlight show
Love's counties under lifting mist,
The body's imminent tableau.

A PHOTOGRAPH AND SWANS

THE pleasure boats are in,
And the wintering swan
Floats on his heated reservoir at ease;
The carrousel and all
Are long put by, since fall,
Corrupt with cold, has caught the failing trees.

These tender ruins try
The memory:
And we are walking there again, and the swans
Are there, and there the lake
Winks back my tremoring look,
While the sun across that waterscape still shines.

This dark intrudes; I turn.
Now must I learn,
In spite of dead leaves, to hold you distantly,
To blur and to reshape
Your memory, to keep
This photograph, nor any white swan see.

A LETTER

A DAY was nothing until this; words went
Like horns through traffic, like the instant birds;
A day was dormant, yet-to-be-danced among
The sudden neon furniture and books.

It was that intricate familiar thing
When, coughing like the French ambassador,
The postman said his phrase about the rain
And went undeviating through the door.

O, if I wanted legacies, a poem,
An invitation to the dance, or hoped
For declarations of a stranger's love,
My fingers burst like matches on your name.

If it is later now, if the rain has stopped,
If no one dressed in seaweed lurches in
Like some surprised Ophelia with green hands,
I covet reason but for truth like this:

There is communication on the earth
As quiet as the opening of a wing;
There is a wine of choice, and we who drink
Touch all our future to that emphasis.

A LOVE SONG FOR ASH WEDNESDAY

DARLING, our dust,
Which death with other dust will bed,
On Wednesday last,
When, *mea culpa*, mankind fed
On common matter, common thread,
Went privately instead.

Your shadowed smile
At length in shadow-play crossed mine,
To hold me while
Mouths full of ashes sang Amen
And bone with bone in doom's dustbin
Clapped heartbreak in.

Cold serpents pealed,
Like whistling flutes birds lighted off,
Bare trees grown old
In the dead springtime took new leaf.
For the rest of his long-winded life
About us, death was safe.

His time's to waste
Who will, ere long, make waste of us.
Why, then, this haste
To lay unsettled dust? What use
Do we rehearse, what truth impress
But, naked, nakedness?

[63]

This much is ours
That soon dispersed and much the same
Will crowd, of course,
His subconventions of dark loam;
But upright, quick, far from our home,
Sackcloth wears tiresome.

Wind shall not sift
These well-banked ashes quite so soon.
While time is left,
To sleep supine we'll lay us down
Beside, still prone to entertain,
All ways, what lies between.

V

THE WORM IN THE WHIRLING CROSS

No further, fathering logos, withering son,
Shall I my sense for want of grace confess,
But vouch this matter of decaying green
That with a shark's-tooth grin
Hinges the rooftree of my dwelling place.
Anguish I caught when I walked apple-wise
Shows me forever the first sun I mourn:
Wild Tigris at full spring, giraffes and O,
That waterlogged, fell swoop of genesis.
What excellent ray divines it now? To learn
How leaf's mold burns, I would cross grain with you.
When your all-hallowed dome's dove-tailing brows
Fall to, by inscape clearing manscape new
My groundswelled pride shall greet hailstorm and stress.

I'd east, I'd west, O dark idea of sleep,
If from this long idlesse and chrysalis
You'd spread your birdwise fan of shut third eyes
And on the cryptic idioms of snow
And tumid greensward show
The idols of your night to my idyllic day.
O toward identity
Be witness angel and dark partisan.

Upthrust down trodden bedrock's mighty main,
My slow bones stretched on tide-ledge, bog, and dune;
Time's tanglefoot, blood's vein that gags and blinds
Twin to his hungry intertwining twin,
I brushed big fish and fisted my curled hands
At brute Tyrannosaurus and tit-wren,
Honing the spirit flesh would eat alive,
Until, touched with the phosphor of self-love,
The forebrain glowed and light knew it was light.
Around that influence the flying fox,
Flanked by the archaeopteryx,
Sailed through the gloom, and restless under it
The little eohippus cropped his field;
One weather told the world how it grew old.

Begot in, ah, God's ego we go well
Till, ill begun, O sight begone, we die.
Glow, blind worm, seed of that worm-eaten oak
Whose scattered marrow lines my wailing wall,
Yet from my deathbeds, fly:
For I with ice-capped bee in outcropped lime
Am etched into hard time
Like diamonds trailing shucks of common coal: —
God's chemical to lesser dust withdraws,
His basilisk dissolves, chimerical
Light lacing light, while through frankincensed air's
Pin-pointless more or less,
Downcast, trumped up, the bored archangel blares.

How is it, ghost, that fin by fur I fare
Your Christ-crossed voyage yet arrive still born?
Packed in my brain your rod and sepulcher
Mark the dim stations of the way I come

[68]

Toward my lost other father, my lost home,
Yet wake to find a curling embryo:
But O, perhaps we know —
More than we know. . . . How does the mantis pray?
Does he not fix his dark Silurian eye,
Stark ebony, on the revolving day,
His mechanism pulleyed and well strung,
And with precise antennae cautiously
Tuned all a-twitch to his predaceous wing,
Drink the charged space with vast humility?

   Ice is my sometime high time home, where bone
On cross-bone breeds the issue I would save
Though in my time's sick house I squander it.
So minded may I not, spare head of wit,
By foul means brought to these dead ends alive,
From troubled meanings strike the singleton?
God is the verb by whither out of whence
(Heigh-ho hosanna on Nirvana's couch)
Intransitive, yet active past pretense.
This nothing infinitely out of touch,
Spontaneous mote that kindled waters once,
Spies on the guilt-flecked whites of inner eyes
And drops a saint's-bait hook. "Deliverance,"
My ancient cries, and shakes the astonished trees:
"I found this notion in a lily pond,
And with a riblike wand
Divined it for mine, umbilicus and crown:
Then on the stagnant pond the pregnant sun
Showed one preponderant lily and I knew;
Wherefor my knucklebones cracked in His praise;
And like to like my face looked in His face."

Old adamantine clay, clearly though I hold
Your myth and office, and your fall reflect,
Your matter's seasoned well but not well told.
Before God's creature walked
His fetus somersaulting like a clown
Arrived here upside down;
His question was not, Shall I be foreborne?
But How may I forebear what I am born?
Through the wet nurseries of the fig leaf one
Sweet wind distributed his song and story;
No sooner sung than sorry;
In speaking bush and philosophic stone,
He cut a finite figure twice his size;
The grave stone spoke, a little whittled wood
Grew out of hand and into Paradise;
He thought there were two sides to every grave
Mark of his design, and overweighed with love,
Put out his vessels of propitious blood.

Time-honored, O false fathered, dreaming you,
I fell through swells, ripped tide and undertow,
Ebb following on flow, the blind crab's house
Of furbelow that holds him far below:
"See! Sea-changed one," I said, "how the light goes!"
Alas, a sea horse blue
As silence floating by was all his word;
So we become each other after all
(In time or late, as time alone will tell);
All ways my only now, I said or heard:
"Because I fell what me befalls, I will,
And will withal, in flyblown amber guard
My yard of bones from senseless pyramids!
My word it was crowned the concentric Word

Combustible ditch-water simmered toward,
My fate it was unwound love's fetal cord.
Whirled word! and syllabus of all that hides
Manslaughter, the dog and go and do God
Might from his mill's almighty grindstone free.
Yet I am one. One moves me. None may die;
For all I know, horizons crossing me
My course at three crossroads pike vertical;
O when that cross is twirled, whereon I lie,
My hair and hide bound on the brain-racked wheel
Illusion spins, may fly wherefor and why;
As painted figures on a rolling ball
Show in their turns as one, I shall be whole;
— Yet still this bloodshot globe's an eyeball by
Mind's dead-eye dark blacked out, unless I say."

Goodbye, god-father; sons go on their own
In the long run; farewell, old potentate,
Old lion-heart; though I know woebegone
And prophetless travail avail me nought.
Cast-off of dust, I bolt your five-barred gate
Once more, and clapped anew, through avenues
Of sand-stormed hours spilled time-counterwise,
Fall backward back to the embalming lake
Where cold, infertile, the moon's eye keeps one
Twin cradle with the whole soft seed of man.
O bridegroom floating in the white bride's wake,
O mirror-peeling, moon-appalling face,
Your fire falls, locked antlers in the bough,
As over cowls of snow,
Arising, haloed with hot sapphire and ice,
Firstborn offspring of metamorphosis,
I ride my beast-king Christ through Paradise;

[71]

Yet will taboos their cutthroat totems raise,
And soon in blood-soaked sorrow Sophocles
Will publish my dead issue and its name.
O fatal apple of your father's eye,
At this core of the matter lies your dream.
Ah well, ill-webbed or well this net plots my
Hell-bent heyday — coiled from the eggshell skull,
Foundering truth of that profound doom's day
Dumfounding all, boomeranged bone again,
Whistling fissions howl through God's cracked bowl;
Who loves his life leaves well enough alone,
Holding his tongue at Pentecost of death,
While somewhere shuttling slowly something weaves
For saw-toothed worms his ragbag mummy cloth,
— Sleep soundly, doom's man, sleep, and be dream's child:
— For, when all's twice told, all told we lie cold.

Stone rolling, cocksure morning, show my son,
And eastering, and westering, at full sail,
Touch these cold stones with specular design;
Toward my lean amplitude be bountiful,
With cockerel quill entablature such rule
As will prevail, and fill with blowing grain
The horn that bids the rakish wedding guest;
When worse comes to the worst, at your behest
Let wine-and-water's sons and daughters mix;
Bless, with good-natured artifice and wit,
Hands that would tend minds our mismarriage breaks,
And over guilt-edged beds long overwrought
Hang emblems from your seamless canopy.
Pull the reluctant water-coddled boy
Up by his roots, and shape his fungus foot
This way, and that way, so long as he may

Find his way forward by his afterthought.
Shine, androgyne, old soloist of dawn;
Your forelocked heirs arise, and on death's bane
Their life-spans overarch, where in the world
Inhuman nature bears one human child.

Host to the worm who'll entertain my clay,
I face my love's child on the face of earth;
His eye's all sea as I remember sea
Where swordfish minnows shred God's images;
His song, swan son, pealed from the stripling tree
Fills my last breath whereon his mouth must close;
As the bough burns, the seed explodes in air:
Wherever I walk now, I wake not here.

VI

LA CREAZIONE DEGLI ANIMALI

HERE that old humpback, Tintoretto, tells
Of six days' labor out of Genesis:
Swift from the bowstring of two little trees
Come swans, astonished basilisks and whales,
Amazed flamingos, moles and dragonflies
To make their lifelong helpless marriages;
Time is a place at last; dumb wonder wells
From the cracked ribs of heaven's gate and hell's.

The patriarch in that vicinity
Of bubble seas and eggshell esplanades
Mutters his thunder like a cloud. And yet
Much smaller issues line the palm of God's
Charged hand: a dog laps water, a rabbit sits
Grazing the footprint of divinity.

A NEW ENGLAND SAMPLER

MISS DICKINSON is gone;
Mr. Thoreau has lain
In deeper Concord for
Some fourscore years and more.
*I thought these were the bones
Would rise like tawny pines.*

Cabot came down this way,
Took five redskins away
To show for sixpence in
Alleys Shakespearian.
*I thought these were the bones
Would rise like tawny pines.*

Newport, when Henry James
Was there, smelled of the Thames;
His polished jaw and eye
Furthered the heresy.
*I thought these were the bones
Would rise like tawny pines.*

When Jonathan Edwards went
To live in a Berkshire tent,
The Indians knew the result:

His tongue was difficult.
*I thought these were the bones
Would rise like tawny pines.*

Scholarship and time
Pile books upon their names,
Whose biographies on stone
Are paged by careless rains.
*I thought these were the bones
Would rise like tawny pines.*

THE GIANT TURTLE GRANTS
AN INTERVIEW

How old are you, Old Silence?
  I tell time that it is.
And are you full of wonder?
  Ephemeral verities.
What most do you long for?
  No end to my retreat.
Have you affections, loves?
  I savor what I eat.
Do shellbacks talk to shells?
  Sea is a single word.
Have you some end in mind?
  No end, and no reward.
Does enterprise command you?
  I manage a good freight.
Has any counsel touched you?
  Lie low. Keep quiet. Wait.
Your days — they have a pattern?
  In the degree of night.
Has solitude a heart?
  If a circle has a center.
Do creatures covet yours?
  They knock, but seldom enter.
Have you not once perceived
  The whole wide world is yours?
I have. Excuse me, I
  Stay utterly indoors.

IMPERIAL GESTURE FOR
MARTHA GRAHAM

CLEAR the courtyard circle of its chalky dust,
Draw banners in, and blood-brocaded symbols;
Latch the casements, and in suffocation rest,
Thread afternoon with beads and sweaty thimbles.

Noon's blaze has drained the roses into rags,
Split the dazzling pots, the baking chalice,
Every parched parcel of this ducal space,
The porch, the portal, and the bleached trellis.

While there she dances with her raging shadow,
Singing la la la, then ro co co,
Making of the dust a macabre meadow,
Singing la la la, then shoo shoo shoo.

Like mummies in the camphor-smelling turret,
The ladies of the court look down, cocooned
With butterflies and chafing to be out
Of pressing darkness where they are marooned.

For there she dances with that risqué shadow,
Singing la la la, then shoo shoo shoo,
Making of the court a macabre meadow,
Singing dum dee dee and ro co co.

The vines are snapping like unstranded rope,
The roses drop their petal-papers, nod
Their wiry stems in winds that trail her cape,
For all their coiling roots and thorns are dead.

Yet still she dances with her raging shadow,
Singing dum dee dee and ro co co,
Making of the dust a macabre meadow,
Singing la la la, then shoo shoo shoo.

Though the nervous bean bombard the bloated pod,
The sun retreat, the moon come dripping ice,
Still she dances on the bright compacted mud,
Her palms a-click and her quick feet like dice.

NUNS AT EVE

ON St. Martin's evening green
Imaginary diamond, between
The vestry buttress and the convent wall,
Solemn as sea birds in a sanctuary,
Under the statue of the Virgin they play baseball.
They are all named Mary,
Sister Mary, Mary Anthony or Mary Rose,
And when the softball flies
In the shadow of the cross
The little chaplet of the Virgin's hands
Contains their soft excitements like a house.

A flying habit traces
The unprecedented rounding of the bases
By Sister Mary Agatha, who thanks God
For the easy triple and turns her eyes toward home;
As *Mary, Mother, help me* echoes in her head,
Mild cries from the proud team
Encourage her, and the obliging sun,
Dazzling the pitcher's box
With a last celestial light upon
The gold-spiked halo of the Virgin in her niche,
Leads Sister Mary John to a wild pitch.

Prayer wins the game.
As Sister Mary Agatha comes sailing home
Through infield dusk, like birds fanwise
In the vague cloisters of slow-rising mist,
Winners and losers gather in to praise
The fleetness of a bride of Christ.
Flushed and humble, Agatha collects the bats
And balls, while at her belt
Catchers' and pitchers' mitts
— Brute fingers, toes and gross lopsided heads —
Fumble the ropes of her long swinging beads.

SONG FOR STRANGERS IN WALES

BETWEEN Red Roses and St. Clears
I met an old man all eyes and ears;
Hands trembling twigs, head snowing snow,
He had no mortal place to go
To lay his cheek or say his prayers
Between Red Roses and St. Clears.

Between Red Roses and St. Clears,
"Father," I said, "persuade your tears
Toward one who has sore need of them."
"Son," he replied, "do not condemn
The spittle and phlegm of all these years
Between Red Roses and St. Clears."

Between Red Roses and St. Clears,
Hail-fellow-met, we palmed our fears,
His for the world, mine for me,
Two blossoms on the apple tree,
Then linked our arms and clinked our beers
Between Red Roses and St. Clears.

Between Red Roses and St. Clears
I said so long to his white hairs
And watched him go, humped in his age,

Under the stars and over the bridge.
Nobody knows, nobody cares
Between Red Roses and St. Clears.

Between Red Roses and St. Clears
I skulked for owls and polar bears.
The sun rose sober, as did I.
Something was smoking in the sky:
"Beware yourselves! my dears, my dears,
Between Red Roses and St. Clears."

VISITING CARD FOR EMILY

No chronicle, melody, alarm of strings
Informed our accident of meeting here,
Nor plowed the atmosphere
As if an almanac had so defined
This day, this town, this wind:
Up from the Cape, a lemon morning swings
With acid light for things
Fir-pointed and oblique,
Stains the Berkshires, spreads on woods to seek
Some quiet entrance to the western state
And leave us Emily for intimate.

Hail this acre for a new world's myth,
A gayer dust than all New England's quarry,
Hail this sanctuary;
Our transcendental hostess here resigned
Her concourse with the blind
To lift upon materials of death
Imperial monolith,
In echoing chambers made
Of gems and bones her private balustrade,
Or carved on quietude a spear, a wing;
This acre's measure is a learned thing.

Among the candelabra, high-branched, cold,
This baroque jail of her fine agony,
Silver, mahogany,
Old silence, evident of her, presides:
Its armored air recedes
To such mementos as the mind recalls,
Nor quick hand ever holds,
To such remembrance as
That of Donne, of Blake, and Shelley is.
To this degree is her distinction weighed
Who took the whitest elements to wed.

This hour countered time for us, who must retreat
And force our visions on the temperate east
Where now no sign is passed
That does not speak memorials to her,
Nor arrowing vistas where
She is not ultimate; quick daisies fret
No casual field, nor shut
Their buttons on a hill
But she is imminent and super-real.
How coolly now the failing sun awards
Sweet praise to Emily, her book of words.

not an attitude
but a climate —
   native riviera
   where light, pale but successful, spots
      a lank destroyer stopped in a gorgeous calm,
      or a sharklike sloop.

Nothing predicted
her, unless the
   sea did, tossing, like a
   diamond in Kansas, a mil-
      limeter's labyrinth of coral on the
      tides of Rockaway;

unless another
age did, when, in
   a sky-blue vestal gown
   and ice-blue jockey cap (the stripes
      were meaningless, the sporting kings were dead) she
      rode a merry race

near Paris in the
Degas steeplechase,
   figuratively, of
   course. Vision cracked with a pin, its
      voyages at a standstill, its purposes
      exposed yet honored —

polarities that
span the world, while
   Yankee-jawed camels, the
   chariest most north-of-Boston
      types, scheme through the needle's eye to find, if not
      their proper heavens,

facsimiles there-
of. It is not
   that another couldn't
   match her method of embalming
      mirrors but that, like so much which passes for
      life in Brooklyn, she

happened there first. To
an age of art-
   ifice she brings laurels
   of artifact. How special, then,
      are these few poems of a rectitude so
      insular they will

be saved as saints are
saved whose palms bleed
   annually, because
   like the glass flowers at Harvard
      (lessons in perfect lifelessness) they are what
      they're talking about.

THE GRAVE SONG OF
WYSTAN HUGH AUDEN

CHIPPED angels, just as you knew they would,
Look down all day on the indecent graveyard cats.
    That the conduct of their *grandes affaires*
Would make your thatched roof shake, however,
Was a thought anticipation would not accommodate —
    Like twin Jesuits or green hair.

Still, if winged Hope and bawling Reason,
No more than you, can wholly ban or choose
    This tepid corner for their *mise-en-scène,*
At least the Egyptian gates are closed on time,
The fastidious traffic veiled by sycamores
    And fairly quiet by ten.

O you who taught us Everything and More —
The lusts of the uncivil kidney, the brain's
    Dim anthropophagous
Determination, the childish heart's *Sieg Heil* —
Look down indulgent on the massive ignorance
    Of Elder Statesman and Poor Cuss.

For yours was the impermeable gaze of the Aryan
As, from the marvelous tents of his high camp,
    He watched the Never Quite Rejected
Cavort *en fête* in their all too lucid woods;
To the delectable *panache* of their minor statutes
    You were never madly attracted.

[91]

How unlike us, who, meaning every silly thing we said,
Could neither burke the *angst* of this anarchic age
    Nor to the gruff Almighty Copper
Display the appalling smile of Really Good Behavior.
O Master who, intelligent beyond your generation,
    Was death's-head at its buffet supper,

When beguiling salesmen of the utterly secondhand
Ententes and visions of the Truly Better World
    Unroll their shoddy bills of goods,
Excuse our impulse to the quick deposit, the doomed
Chat at the reluctant door, the self-smirk
    Of self-seeking attitudes.

O when, toward blue eternity's *plage d'or*, we come
Like fretful Grace and her delinquent children,
    Forgive us at that final border.
O do not hold up the passports of our innnocence
But, *cum grano salis*, in our nervous luggage find
    Every little thing in order.

TWELVE OR THIRTEEN WAYS OF
LOOKING AT WALLACE STEVENS

IT is, peut-être, an eye abstract of pomp
And resignation. A scrumptious syllable —
Katchoo! — divining what is sensible.

It holds the loftiest idea of swans —
Not hissing esses, dank feathers in a pool —
But the idea of swans, immiscible.

On a day nauseous with grackles and rabbits
Just so one had seen it. It had not seen one.
The contretemps was no catastrophe.

Pipkin the fond man, gazing, thinks,
"My eye, if it *is* mine, can kindle it."
His ignorance is magnified, rhapsodic.

And yet for him, insipid acolyte,
The moonlight has a mild farewell, ta ta.
He will exist in that beneficence.

To promise everything, and so it does,
To allocate niente, and so it does —
Bad illustrations of divinity.

What is one eye among so many eyes?
A. Jocundus, purple in his grapes.
B. The sternest monitor of metaphor.

The eye, ai-yi, goes round the world,
The world, ai-yi, goes round the eye —
The waltz of the babies of Omaha.

It is, peut-être, une impasse des deux anges,
The one borne downward, cherry-ripe,
The one toward heaven.
                Pure.
                    Gruff.

W<small>HEN</small>
       Doctor
Edith (Hon. D. Litt. Leeds, Hon. D. Litt. Durham)
Descends in Mayfair from her brougham
Tall as a chimney stack,
Her
      straight
           back
Encased in a pelisse as black
As cloven Lucifer's silk sack,
She
Enters a bluestockinged club
And, through the Grub Street antics
Of best-selling Corybantes
Who
From castles and from hovels
Meet to contemplate their novels,
Elicits sudden hushes
'Mongst the pudding-colored plushes.

Her hat is a black wheel,
With six spokes of tempered steel,
From her swan's neck hang medallions
Brought from Tenerife in galleons,

And her fingers are afire
With cut amethyst, sapphire,
When
At ease with duke and Cockney,
A transmigratory Procne,
She folds her flutt'ring wing and tail
And perches on the Chippendale.

Yet in that grace marmoreal,
Mantilla'd and Escorial,
Deep
As the sea
On which sails the slant Chinee
She
Sounds the mad note of Ophelia,
The sad organ of Cecilia,
The song of Dian as, a-hunting,
She outraced the brute and grunting
Dryads of the lewd and moody wood.
Up to no good!
She orders Martinis
And quick as Houdinis
The waiters in gaiters return in a trice.
They know as well as we
It
  was
    she
Who took a verse a-dying
And with her sweet bazooka
Sent its fusty fragments flying.
Encircled by critics
Benign and mephitic,

[96]

By poets long dead and *nouveaux*,
She blesses, caresses, and what she dismisses
She kills with the dart of a *mot.*
So.

At lunch as the bards nip
Mutton and parsnip,
The homage like *fromage*
Comes in with the fruit.
"Ah, laureate lady,"
Says one as he reaches
Toward apples and peaches,
"Once cottoned and bent to
Your tones *quattrocento,*
Who then could descend to
The deserts of prose?"

       "You are sweet," says she
        (Purring and stirring the oolong),
"To admit you've been smitten
         By these bits that I've written."
        "Not at all," says he,
"For the charm, don't you see,
Is a matter, *au fond,* of British *esprit:*
When
Bertie and Harry,
Dirty and hairy,
Loaf by the docks of the gull-splattered sea
In Plymouth and Harwich and Dover,
Who's to oppose their sordid repose,
Who's to amuse them but you?"
        "Lunch is over!" says she.

LITTLE ELEGY FOR GERTRUDE STEIN

Pass gently, pigeons on the grass,
For where she lies alone, alas,
Is all the wonder ever was.

Deeply she sleeps where everywhere
Grave children make pink marks on air
Or draw one black line . . . here to there.

Because effects were upside down,
Ends by knotty meanings thrown,
Words in her hands grew smooth as stone.

May every bell that says farewell,
Tolling her past all telling tell
What she, all told, knew very well.

If now, somehow, they try to say —
This way, that way, everywhichway —
Goodbye . . . the word is worlds away.

Come softly, all; she lies with those
Whose deepening innocence, God knows,
Is as the rose that is a rose.

VII

ARCHITECT, LOGICIAN

ARCHITECT, logician, how well the snail
Narrates his tenuous predicament!
Knit with fragility, its echoing cowl
Enchants the space wherein he's pent,
Yet holds his heart like water in a bowl.

Like those who temper opal for a house,
A wise man keeps the cosmos in his skull
Rimmed with a box of sound where every day
Repeats his wishing yet confirms him whole.
As flesh grows merry in its neutral shell,
Beware the pleasures of small bones that fit
Elbow to brow when the design's not whole;
Each hauls his house; the trick's to live in it.

FACES, FACES

I go toward some green land
Unpainted with the manlike face of God
Where, each for its own sake,
The mast-and-spar, the cliff and thunderhead,
The cabbage, wolf's-jaw and the stoic rock
Across my blind foresight
Ride on a field of light;
I follow shadows towering from spilled shades
That from the first, all ghost,
Charged with their dark my dearest neighborhoods;
At last, so self-possessed,
I take my view in hand.

As in the fluted wind
Jaws long locked and silent sing through bones,
The stare of nothingness
Enchants and haunts the face of God man wants
To mask Allhallows with boys' mysteries;
As time eats time like sand,
Nets of a world's wind bind
The death's-head moth, the coral and the clock.
Such faces God's face marries,
Spawning new martyrs on the bridal rack
From which the child of space is
Lifted in blood and burned.

Have left and leave now ever
Sleeping head on elbow-cradled arm
To meet the window-face,
The foundling brainstone, the benign glowworm
And, far from houses, the fog-featured rose;
Down, down live diver
In his blue free-swimming fever
I kiss the fathering faces of us all
That, soluble as flesh,
Appear and fade like figures on a shell
The far-flung rains shall wash
And winds shall topple over.

Mystery, like a glass bird in a box,
Assails the space that yet encloses it;
Remote, at ease come cage or paradox,
Yonder the pure shapes of mere wonder float.

Wonder, strange pond where drift the dim, sad swans,
And the ancient turtle paddles in the lily bed,
Lays ghost by Holy Ghost; while through that once
Known water's hyssop of puerperal blood,
Evil the mystery, feathering a thought,
Rattles like God its little bonewhite foot.

GLORIOUS VICTORY OF THE SLOOP MARIA

HER breastbone bent toward victory, breeze-blue
Maria skirts the offshore barber poles
    And, like a page of music blown,
Slides home all angles with her face-down crew.

First on the line and first across the water,
Maria starts the whole flotilla tooting,
    Circles the candy lighthouse twice,
Then slows at ease in zephyrs of applause.

So glorious it was, all afternoon.
Yet what, in telling, dips as bowsprits do
    Or plunges those white straining manes
Below, above that spindrift furbelow?

To try the wings of summer, summer gone,
The seascapes splash on clubhouse walls
    When the wind blows or does not blow.
The moment undermines the framed memento,

Because Maria floats in dead seas now,
A lolling memory of a victory past,
    Her glorious mainsail stricken short
Between the gun and the far-off retort.

THE BLUE SWAN FROM WYOMING
TO PERU

THE blue swan from Wyoming to Peru
Resumes, one feather lost, his cold patrol;
Upswept at times, at times volplaning low,
My soaring sailor on his snow-wide sail
Arrives nowhere; his sorry shadow hangs
Nightlong on rock, and daylong lines his wings.

Captivity of self, like the guitar's
Abundant silences, attracts the wind
Put forth for sorrow, the grief that wears
Only the landscape proper to its kind.
This folded bird, for all he bear another,
Endures a blizzard in one falling feather.

APPROACHING by the gate (Class of '79,
All dead), the unimpressed new scholars find
Halls of archaic brick and, if it is April,
Three dazzling magnolias behind bars, like lions.

Unsettling winds among the pillars of wisdom
Assure them of harmonious extremes,
However academic. The bells, in key,
Covered with singing birds, ring on the hour.

Towering, but without aspiration, the campanile
Is known to sway an inch in a high wind;
But that, like the statue's changeable complexion,
Is natural. To find the unnatural,

Gradually absorb the industry
Of ten o'clock: the embryo pig slit through
With the proper instruments by embryos;
And Sophocles cut, for speed, with a blue pencil.

Prehensile sophomores in the tree of learning
Stare at the exiled blossoming trees, vaguely puzzled;
The lecturer, especially if bearded,
Enhances those druidical undertones.

What is the terminus of books? sing the birds.
Tell us about Sophocles! cry the trees.
And a crazy child on roller skates skates through
The campus like a one-man thunderstorm.

THINK OF THAT PLACE

THINK of that place among all buried places,
Hideout of dog and angel: there children stand
Eternal, mindless, in the bandaged dress
Old scarecrows hurl, all sleeves, against the wind;
Dead-white, with sad top-heavy heads entwined,
Of love the monuments, love-locked they fall,
Root, rib and swaddling cerement one grave,
One tidal wave the fishing moon's long pull
Shores like a cockleshell but cannot save.

Sun of their sleep, the good year's native light
Tunes the young engines of earth's changelessness,
And through the world's veined head, all moss and eyes,
Mortality unwinds — night after night
On mandrake roots to scream, half man, half tree,
Saying to scarecrow children, Wait for me.

BY GLORY, SAID THE GREEK

BY Glory, said the Greek, and omens fell
In bird-gut alphabets on the whirlpool —
Lightly the zeta floated, lightly the psi,
Lightly the hollow amens of prophecy.

Riddled and reft, poor raddled skeletons
Enter the flotsam delta time discards;
At long length, on the esplanade of bones,
Designs of Greeks cross-stitch the songs of birds.

SPEECH OF THE WEDDING GUEST

O RANDOM dove that binds its kissing kin,
   Entwinèd bird, most linked with written gold,
By this discretion among choices be
   The severing wind that doth unmarry me.

For singleness as witness to the fact
   Knows the full price, yet wary of the cost,
Makes benedictions with the best of heart,
   Blessing the sea by which it stands apart.

So, soft aloft and lighting, dithering bird,
   This ritual of love and goods demands
Meticulous attendance to make mute
   The hither and yawning of the mourning flute.

By your good office, two once met as two
   Are joined and doubled to become unique;
Yet would you be incautious to outstay
   The fluttering homiletics of the day.

As night falls to renew the whispering green
   Of the first fell garden where your feathers shone,
Be off, pert package, to your own dovecote
   And give free ribbon to their chariot.

[110]

Be watchful of my dark; I will watch yours.
For by this mating we are met alone,
Cohabitors of nought or, if we please,
Of furnished rooms in the antipodes.

When, bursting from a bell, you wheel on streets
Mosaic with confetti, blinds still drawn,
Brood not that, heedless of your hermitage,
A rumpled sheet has ratified a pledge.

Yours was the moment frozen in the dance.
Another music carries you away.
O in that measure bless what you can bless
And light, for my part, upon singleness.

VIII

Translations
from the Poetry of
Jorge Carrera Andrade

AUTHOR'S NOTE: I am indebted to Louis d'Almeida for major assistance in making the translations from the poetry of Jorge Carrera Andrade and to the Bollingen Foundation for a grant under which they were undertaken.

LIFE OF THE CRICKET

An invalid since time began,
he goes on little green crutches,
stitching the countryside.

Incessantly from five o'clock
the stars stream through
his pizzicato voice.

Hard worker, his antennae,
dragging like fish-lines,
troll the high floods of air.

At night a cynic,
he lies inert in his grass house,
songs folded and hung up.

Furled like a leaf,
his folio preserves
the records of the world.

WINDY WEATHER

I HAVE a professor of classical literature
who has taught me to hate the written word:
He is the country wind, the sweet old man
whom farmers call Don Ventura.

Don Ventura's a maniac. He goes out at dawn,
searching through the limp damp grass
for the yardstick of integrity in knowledge.
He roams the forest, croaking to himself.

Kneeling foliage give him their blessings.
The millpond roars and the waters tremble.
Later, in the quiet of a tree, Don Ventura
is a sage priest dictating his lessons.

He reads the forecast of rain in clouds,
and calls at every door to leave his warnings.
Neighbors with an ear to the ground
begin shouting: *Here comes Don Ventura!*

IT RAINED ALL NIGHT

IT rained all night:
the pears have got stuck in the ground
and the cabbages are prostrated
like abbesses.

Of such things speaks
the bird on the window sill,
the bird who is the journal
of morning in this country.

Outside: confusions.
Let us rise from our warm bed.
The rain has washed our lives
as it would rinse a cabbage.

NOTES FROM A PARACHUTIST

I FOUND only two birds and the wind,
clouds with their maps rolled up,
flowers of smoke that searched the skies
as, bundled tight, I made my slow descent.

Because I come from the high heavens
of old prophecies and hymns,
an emissary uniformed in a white sheet
and bear a whole supply of lives and deaths,

I walk down the sky as the sun does.
I moisten the patient eyelids
of those who wait for me: I have
followed the freshets of light and rain.

Kind shrub, protect me.
Earth, tell your wet furrows to welcome me,
and have the newly fallen log
instruct me in fervor and how to lie inert.

Farmers of Europe!
I come in the name of bread, of the world's mothers,
of all beheaded whiteness:
the heron, the lily, the lamb, snow.

[118]

My arm is powered by murdered cities,
mutilated families dispersed over the earth,
blond children and bright provinces that burn
in the dark centuries of blood.

Farmers of the world: I descend
like a white rainspout, like an airborne medusa.
I bring not only lightning and death sentences,
I bring the crops of a green hill.

I bring a time of harvest without soldiers;
In the hour of the night's defeat, I'll put,
once more, a light in every window.
I am the newest angel of the century.

Although I citizen the cloudy air,
by the earthly blood that courses in my veins
I know the path that leads to every house,
the road that flows beneath all moving vehicles,

the running water that pretends to be
the same swift water you have just passed by,
the land of animals, of vegetables with tears,
where, with my outspread hands, I'll summon day.

MY MOTHER'S SECOND LIFE

I HEAR about me your familiar step,
the pacings of clouds or a slow river;
your gentle pride and humble majesty
subjecting me to an eternal domination.

Over unforgotten reaches of pale time,
over green families prostrate on the earth,
over discarded costumes, the sad wardrobes
of a rainy country, you reign quietly.

You walk among insects and mushrooms,
your laws control my hands each day;
your voice runs furtively in mine
dissolving its ashes and base metals.

Compass of my journey in the world.
Origin of my blood, source of my destiny,
When earth had drawn your face to his,
I awoke surprised to find I was alive.

And I tried to break down invisible doors,
a prisoner who raged in vain.
On ropes of sobs I tried to hang myself;
Calling after you, I was swamped in dreams.

But you found new life inside me.
I feel you gently, gently breathing,
and so surmise a celestial order in
the sweet things guided by your hands.

You give full substance to the morning sun,
and with an old solicitude you wind me
in your bright, weightless cloak,
cool as cockerel morning and its shadows.

You count the liquid notes of insects and birds,
the sweetness of the world that comes to me;
your tender signals point the way I go;
in solitude I speak in your occult language.

You move in all my gestures, all my silences.
Over my shoulder you issue your commands.
When night soaks up all colors,
emptiness breathes your infinite presence.

I hear inside me your small prophecies,
and, by my side through all my vigils,
you still advise me on events, inscrutable codes,
the genesis of stars, the age of plants.

My heart in heaven, live, live without years.
My own first blood, my own first light,
may your immortal inspiration in all things
like a vast chorus surround me and sustain me.

NOTHING BELONGS TO US

Every day, the selfsame tree surrounded by
his family of green rumors . . .
Every day, clocking its piece of time,
the pendulum swings in the shade . . .

The heavy river deals its transparent deck.
Silence investigates a nearby noise.
With small and tender fingers
the seed tears off his linen swaddling clothes.

No one knows why the birds exist,
or the cask of wine, or the full moon,
or the poppy that burns itself alive,
or the harp's wife, happy prisoner.

So one must dress in water, gentle fabrics,
in things invisible and comforting,
and shave with the ineffable softness of doves,
of rainbows and of angels.

So one must pan the meager gold of day,
counting his nuggets in a crippled wind
that wrecks his ships while night approaches
like a captain of dark tribes.

[122]

Then, Heaven, you speak up:
your lights illuminate a dark metropolis;
torch-bearing populations march
and silently, indifferently, look down.

All forms seem vain and loose as dust:
the boy who lies a statue in his crib,
the woman who has two bird hearts,
clandestine death disguised as an insect.

Dead man, you fall, a broken cage,
a mutilated shell,
a spider monstrous and lime-colored,
and in your falling cover the whole world.

The buried dead become a brotherhood,
the Order of the Troglodytes.
Is death the ultimate poverty,
or the reconquest of the original kingdom?

Man, nurtured on years, on women's bodies,
at God's urging you will kneel.
Only the useless memory of things
will warm your empty hands.

PROMISE OF RIO GUAYAS

ENDLESSLY, you put out to sea,
Rio Guayas, loaded with horizons
and the lazy ships that climb
your crystal waves and watery heights.

Running in your path, time itself
dissolves in your smashed waters.
The tropical day that won't come back
rolls in your furrows toward oblivion.

Indifferently you watch the years
that burn out gradually,
the slow migrations of the ages,
O shepherd of levees and cities!

The freighters, the destroyers,
the explorers, the adventurers —
you have escorted them to shore,
or in your mobile graveyard drowned them.

Your tranquil flowing is disturbed
by nothing but your own still scream,
or by your dreams: the underwater plant,
sly fish that are both quick and lazy.

Always inspecting your properties,
you count cattle, haciendas, green grottoes.
Meandering in your solitudes,
you lose yourself in the damp rushes.

Husbandman, you drag the loam
that fertilizes banks
populated by trees and houses
standing on wooden stilts.

The palpitation of your flowing heart
measures the beat of everything:
the sugar cane, and the sleepy alligator —
dragon from another age.

By night, a shadow on your banks,
the buccaneer, defunct, still makes his tracks,
and a blue canoe, fishing for stars,
paddles illegal cargo down the dark.

Memory, river, flowing solitude,
you move, yet always stay, urgently
the same, the same, yet different,
running away from yourself.

To your water spaniels and foam spaniels
I throw my false exotic vesture;
to your liquid promise I deliver myself;
I believe in your refreshing words.

O, river, captain of great rivers!
Your vast, unceasing flow
is like my blood, filled with ships
arriving and departing endlessly.

IX

PRAGUE

I THINK of Prague, the gargoyles dark and glum,
I feel the waltzes halted and behold
That monstrous city cold.

The ranges of the iron trees extend
Across the ancient distance and beyond
Still centuries of silent halls,
Bright swords inert in scabbards,
Ecclesiasts' cold cupboards,
Lean windows draping dust against the sun.

Where some philosopher of evening lifts
His mournful eyes to monuments,
There, defamed by pigeons and bereft
Of any earthly radiance,
The parchment past and its high glories blow.

And far across tall battlements the town
Submits to darkness and the scenic night;
Cold sentinel stars are bright, and bright
The river where a suicide is found.

A child will strangle in his giant dreams,
Some housewife to the grinning soldier come,
Some poet break his knuckles on the page,
A singer crumple on an empty stage.

I think of Prague, the night's machinery done,
That fatal city in the naked dawn,
Historic and alone.

THE ALPS

Look down from Switzerland, and weep for sight,
Recounting the southern pleasance of Champagne,
And the painted Nordic plain
Submissive now to policies of night;
Where Paris sleeps in sleeplessness anew,
And Rome is ruins with a clown for keep,
Look down and weep,
Since every Gothic tale is now come true.

The bathers on the Adriatic shore
Come in a little early from the waves;
A blond announcer raves
Over the rainy suppertime at Tours.
In Bohemian dusk, a lone woodcutter turns
One more Madonna for his endless shelf,
Useless himself,
While in his palm the bread of anger burns.

The crafts of simple men, instructed arms,
Survive in corners like neglected snow;
When the arch-conquerors go
From door to door with bludgeoning alarms,
Accomplishment is secretive; the voice
Of quartered sorrow can defy
A narrowing eye,
Keeping its wisdom for kinsmen of choice.

Where freedom is an art whose laws remake
The shape of equity, whose masterpiece
Is triumph and release
Of power in the heart to build or break,
The temporary artisans of war
Keep bootless tenancy; the hands of the free
Work silently;
Their eyes are calm, their gifts superior.

Look down from Switzerland at chill of night:
The closing bell in the Louvre on the Seine
Disbands the day again,
And on the Dutch lowlands, in vaporous light,
With lavish arms the windmills swing for none;
The shadows of the Matterhorn come down
On the last Swiss town,
And racing over the slopes, the crazy sun.

FOR MY PUPILS IN THE WAR YEARS

To hold to a congress of books when news of death
Fools with the odd chance of your happiness
Is an old and academic idea of truth;
And yet, in the small matter of a page,
Though you are young and centered otherwise,
The instructions of the dead attest your privilege.

Turning their difficult honors in your hands
Like curators with vases, your eyes reprove
Their radical loves and their extravagance
Of spirit under the brightness of dubious gods;
For yours is the climate of a budding grove
In whose dissolving summer learned impasse fades.

Surely the world's not worthier for facts
In a conqueror's litany of taken places
Or a magnate's success. Though a time like yours elects
Impoverished images to classic fame,
In the narrowing plurality of choices
The arch and ruined porch shall be your home.

Yet, since greatness is unfinished and somewhat foolish
In its dead pretensions, you are not involved;
Romantic agonies become your lavish
Idea of a child playing bride on rainy days,
Or the valentine mystery that was never solved
Until you were older, and had moved to another house.

When rebels ride to action, you remain.
For all the anger of your innocence,
Accomplished and free, they will ride back again.
Their guilt is brave, and when you can believe it,
With a cold grace you will take their adult hands,
For there is nothing to learn about death but how to
      achieve it.

THE shifty limpet on his rocky shore
Contrives a conch to make life possible,
And the unbelievable giraffe achieves
A dainty salad from the lissom tree;
Pretending he is flora in the pond,
A silly fish will emulate a frond
To trick the appetite that savors him;
A rabbit in the snow will do the same.

Like tinted views from a dismantled fair,
These illustrations fail, being outworn;
Who would erect a summerhouse of myth
To shade him from the elements of love
Is naked of resource; since love like fate,
Omnipotent and unregenerate,
Keeps calendars that are a joke of time,
The newest grief retells the oldest theme.

Since war, the matter of a generation,
Blunts as it must the savior and the fool,
Fathers and sons in terror worlds apart
Communicate with pity and bare signs;
The accurate bombs that scatter sanity,
The child of Guernica who cannot see
That innocence is death, acquaints me now;
I have learned armor I would disavow.

What grace survives the city's glass and stone,
What facet points the cosmopolitan?
To eke a diamond from its mineral floor
Earth rakes its faculty for quake and tide;
Yet in the city's blaze the millions go
From crib to crypt, nor any gem to show.
Ah, there the heart of man knows less itself
Than the least pink shell upon a watery shelf.

Like feathers on a swan, indifference coats
The reptile remnant of our primacy;
Debauched of tongue in time's slow sabotage,
Both tragedy and outrage come to ash;
Then is the heart adaptable to death.
And creatures who employ the earth, and breathe
The vivid air, ascend, superior;
Who comes to his instruction, stays to fear.

The sun of Genesis is shining still,
Though God is shifted to his place in time;
May evil, here, pace like the captured leopard
Where the good contends dynastically with good;
May earth in its success provide for all
Who lack the logic of the sorry snail,
Who die without a candle, or remain
To citizen the natural state of man.

WINTER TERM

THE sun cracks down on Cambridge like a voice
Where Henry James lies coiled upon the hill;
Held with the sparrows to a winter's choice,
The scholars turn a yellow chronicle
Or cut for Conway with the ski-slung boys;
Hearselike, the afternoon deserts the sill
And, faultlessly, with taller shadows now,
Our Ptolemaic corner sifts the snow.

Designed to pocket whimpering Cicero
And the electric eyes of Marx, this hall
Presumes in hooded prescience to know
The mortal fracas that involves us all;
In diplomatic syllables to show
That all is folly and mercurial,
That death, in masque and matter, has not changed
Since Alexander to his India ranged.

Our world is flame, and if we prove its loss
In burrowed rooms among the curious deer
Or, disenchanted, where the Southern Cross
Is hung with searchlights, lotuses, and fear,
Time, whose complete emotion is remorse,
Will lay our misbegotten legend bare:
This is our house so threatened by mere snow,
These are the features only futures know.

THE NEUTRAL MAN

You too have moved, your gestures bent with elegies
Among the sad displacements of the late known world,
Life in your hands, strict defeat in your eyes.

The metaphor is your apology; your days withhold
From happy accidents of chance or formal choice
The soft excitements of cut glass and old gold,

Pictures of living in whose symmetric ease
Anarchy is canceled while the past, a perfect waltz,
Revolves among politer melodies.

Walking in streets your interest, cosmopolitan though false,
Wilts in the imposition of faces and you are lost.
Like the hero tricked by legend you are someone else.

Nevertheless, your presence at the charity is missed
When, encountering a sad dog or a bright child,
You hail the first taxi and go home depressed.

Something alive pursues, something recalled
From the flowered panels of the third-floor rooms
Where the rocking-horse ran and stories were told

In the space between bedtime and the darkening faces and
      dreams.
Mixing a drink, tuning the radio to Bach,
You ride the ghostly hazards of difficult themes

Untouched; but the sulking dog on the boulevard wakes
You, or the child's fierce joy, and you turn
To the highball gone watery and the radio's stale jokes.

Portraits are mirrors, you think, and if you mourn
It is not waste eminence that claims your grief
Nor the uncompromised eye of the child wherein you learn

Wish and the sudden capture of dead belief;
Though museums have taken your life in the shapes of death
And battlefields your death in the awkward shapes of life,

Your whitening hands, so long withdrawn from both,
Ache with their ambitions . . . A stranger in the late streets,
Drunk, assaulting an obdurate doorway like a moth,

Grants you a moment of unimpeachable anger; but he re-
      treats,
Worn out and reasonable, cheating even your pointless rage;
You draw the blinds and put on all the lights.

Trapped in a looking-glass, but full of improbable courage,
With two bare hands you stand alone;
You achieve that fiction of a lion, king in his cage.

But you have kept irony, at least, and the disguise comes
      down,
For it is all happening somewhere else for real.
Without soliloquies, your classmates take a worthless town

In the tall grass of the tropics; though hundreds fall,
Death is the instance of the unequivocal, they had expected
    no less.
You light a cigarette and flick the match farewell.

Yet morning comes among accumulated elegies
And in their curious circling you hear gunshot and child's-
    play;
You go to the window, and it is neither Monday nor dooms-
    day,
With life in your hands, strict defeat in your eyes.

A SALIENT OF WAR

IN time's unconscious shadow and return,
Turning its flames impartially through leaves,
Cathedrals and deep seas, our only sun
Contrives to shepherd us in days of love
And nights of music full as heart will bear.
Waking, walking through those early palaces
The frost erects among familiar branches,
We know by small traditions how the dark
Is spooling in its net the single spears
Of palms, the flashing tips and blue plateaus
Of ice, the soldier's memories of home.

This incident of war that sifts our will
And pulls apart the wide community
Of nakedness is war against itself.
Its purpose has no parallel on hillsides
Melting the sense with tangled arms of foam,
Nor on the adolescent greens where men
Quite naturally throw off their orchard wreaths
To learn the weather and the facts of love.
Because our memories are mutual,
The world is webbed with veins, and moves
Below its surface like a beating heart.

[140]

Not Plato in his universal jail,
Nor glum Napoleon, Emperor of Snow,
Escapes the fine equation so long joined.
The balance is much tried; our records tell
How the excellent corrupt Marquis, the Saint
With sparrows on his fingers, conquistadors
To margins of the mind that blaze, or clap
The senses in a cold paralysis,
Even the physicians with mechanical third eyes,
Have all come back. In such rich agony
Our skeletons and embryos embrace.

The sun survives, and many definitions
Meaning wonder, meaning more than words
May say. The sea is one, and when we sleep
We sleep upon those shores where darkness is
Discriminately wary of our need
To make, of what we know and wish, our dreams.
In the great equity of daylight and dark,
There will be space for many errors more,
And time to marry what we were and are;
The burning years, like letters overseas,
Make splendid our impossible desires.

THE GARDEN IS POLITICAL

THE garden is political,
Nor may the moody eyes
Of larkspur, zinnia, phlox
Stare that manifest horror down.

Nor will percussive rain come down,
Exciting, quick to change
Flower to essence, essence to flower,
As though the planted headlines

Were a row of four-o'clocks, not headlines,
As though the garden were
A progeny of earth
And not a mask for tragedy.

O, no, garden is tragedy
Up to its generous eyes,
Its sensual order, its élan.
The whole beguiling summer burns

With guilty pleasure, gaily burns,
Waltzes and rounds before
The glimmering imminence of guns.
People like headstones walk

Among the twilit hedges, walk
Slow-motioned, fearing the sudden
Scream, the mutilated body,
Headless, under the leaves.

The lisp and grinning of the leaves
Lasts all the dripping night;
Even the illiterate snake must know
The garden is political.

GUNNERY PRACTICE

IT is always there, rattling the teacups at four,
Tilting the sea gull on his favorite perch,
Twitting his gaudy eye. But in the town,
Well used to it, bread is delivered as usual.

Casual week-enders and furlough brides express
A barbed impatience at its thoughtlessness
And snap a flower's neck or steal a kiss
To scatter the dark shock with countershock.

Shaking the smooth midsummery ocean,
Invisible convulsions mumble in space
Like answering Jehovah. For one wide moment
The ragged flags of panic skitter in the air.

Carefully, though, the embarrassed gull rearranges
His feathers and his nerves, the maiden aunt
With valor pours five cups, and the soldier's girl
In the soldier's hat races to the bandstand.

Fondly the mellowing sun comes down, tracing
The shoreline with its burning pencils, tipping
The lightly balanced shell; and what,
In other times, was privilege for love

Of seascapes or girls is shadow and suspicion.
The evenings are private with but a little laughter;
Songs on a sea-warped piano, perhaps, will sound
Between the soft topple and recess of waves,

Giving sentiment a small identity
While slow tides like unanswered questions withdraw,
And the time is unresolved in the quietude of guns,
And the lights go down like suns drowned in the sea.

EVERY ROOM IS A PLACE TO DIE IN

IT all depends
On baby's stocks and bonds
When on the town in one-night stands

You trace and retrace
The Stations of the Cross,
Blues Alley and Dementia Place,

Involved among
A straight-faced *Sturm und Drang*
Whose echo kids you with a ding and dong

From the Elephant Bar
To Ciro's and from there
To the black house with the red door.

All at once
You know your innocence
When, like a traveling audience,

Faces on a bus
Find you hilarious
For tripping when you try to cross.

When traitorous lights
Dissolve, shuttling your wits
To a soft-shoe routine, you start

From the Elephant Bar
To Ciro's and from there
To the black house with the red door.

On the escalator step
The one lover you'd keep
Moves down when you are moving up.

Behind plate glass
Among small merchandise
You meet, perhaps, the timeless face

Whose easy eyes
Are full of promises
Until, controlled and calm, she goes —

So casually
Aware of your hot eye
She might be Egypt to your Antony.

Fall-guy and hero
Of still another sorrow,
You make your retreat as straight as an arrow

From the Elephant Bar
To Ciro's and from there
To the black house with the red door.

[147]

Nobody knows
How every quick one goes
Incongruously counterwise

To your intent.
It is not that you want
The courage of lions, but that restraints

Of earlier wounds
Have put you at loose ends;
You always take the long way round

From the Elephant Bar
To Ciro's and from there
To the black house with the red door.

Worst is your notion
Of sensitive resignation
Between the highball and the ocean.

Best is murder
Of custodians of disorder,
Night clerk, doorman, and head waiter.

But the night is as black
And wet as the arching back
Of a fish, and nothing comes to take

Your kiss of doom
But an empty taxi from
The late show at the Cancer Room.

Hung-up and sad
But quickly comforted,
You follow where slick shadows lead

From the Elephant Bar
To Ciro's and from there
To the black house with the red door.

It falls away,
Your wherefor and your why,
And what was incontestably

The time to break
Through time leaves but your weak
Inscrutable cold hands that crack

A roving fly
Or lift a daiquiri
To a mirrored stranger's half-shut eye

From the Elephant Bar
To Ciro's and from there
To the black house with the red door.

X

AT THE AIRPORT

HERE, at the airport, waiting,
Watching the schedule by
The opulent calm of a match,
I think: the cold, unpeopled stars,
This hutch of night that wears
A floodlight for an eye,
Have turned against my hope.

When silence broadens: swinging,
Whipped by the wind, the little
Zeppelins report a change;
And from the glassy tower goes
Immediately its subtle news:
Over the moonlight lakes
Whose wings? Whose ancient name?

On margins of the field, cattle
Make their slow and noiseless rounds,
Imprinting daisies or
A singular cleft hoof in mud;
Degenerate, soft-eyed, they plod
Without expectancy;
Sometimes, even, they sleep.

[153]

A signal's up! The humming
Imminence of wings
Berates the thoughtful ear;
I underline my schedule with
A fingernail; across the path
Of light, and lazily,
The great eyes land with pride.

All those I've loved in any
History have come;
Their presence, like a wreath
Of pain, sits coldly on my skull;
Puzzled, resigned to good or ill,
Yet fearing recognition,
I watch them evilly.

Do I dare to greet them, calling
"This is the place, this is
The one who telegraphed?"
Emerging single file, they seem
Like statues scissored from a dream,
Except that in their eyes
The past has turned to stone.

I turn into the City;
Let them wonder who it was
That brought them here, who called
Across the distances as if
Their presence meant his very life;
The City is more kind
With stranger citizens.

Now when I hear my pillow
Hum with those approaching wings,
I remember how they came
Out of the sky that lyric night;
Only a ghost would choose to wait,
Among the quiet cattle,
Their coming down again.

TALKING TO THE AZORES

YOUR look of dying patience tells it all:
the world is underworld. Again, again,
your sea-birds riddle my bad dreams; again,
watching without needing to, I feel
the awful shadow of the actual.

Your fields are tilted, every way is down
to waters trying always to climb up.
I want to shut my eyes. I can't believe
your villages that look like strung-out teeth,
your dead moon mountains, your slow smoke-ring clouds.

So many legends! So few monuments!
Where's the mad horseman pointing a new world?
The saint who, beached upon a sleeping whale,
claimed a new island for the Church of Rome?
They were all wrong. You are not stepping stones.

Linked bow to stern, like infant elephants,
squat fishing boats go loping round your shores
at work that somehow has the look of pleasure.
Your weather eyes are doomed to separateness,
yet on a clear day you surprise each other.

Any old map has found a place for you.
God knows, I have to see you when I look.
Show me the volcano that you hatched last year,
show me the stubborn parishes that cling
like oysters to your dripping undersides.

It is all too late. I say things in my sleep.
There must be nothing, nothing at all between us.
You are wholly imaginary! My great ship,
scrawling big esses off the coast of Pico,
etches on slate its cut-glass signature.

SONG FROM THE OUTER OFFICE

THE 'Sconset rose is on the fence
   The snail is on the rose,
The summer sea's mild influence
   Bids me discard my shoes,
But where shall I go this summer?

The *Island Queen* at Woods Hole waits;
   At Ipswich wait the clams;
The Berkshires hark to the first flutes
   Of Beethoven and Brahms.
But where shall I go this summer?

Off Kennebunk the black whales wheeze
   As, perilous and forlorn,
From widow's walks landladies gaze
   And pray for my return.
Oh, where shall I go this summer?

Saltboxes far beyond my means
   Are still for rent in Truro;
There's Sun Deck space aboard the *Queens,*
   But Europe I'm not sure of. Oh,
Where shall I go this summer?

[158]

Sometimes Quebec still calls me back!
    Would the Hamptons help my status?
Would Maine be the wrong step to take?
    Hyannis a hiatus?
Oh, *where* shall I go this summer?

The Thousand Islands should be counted;
    Lake George should be canoed;
If Provincetown's half what it's painted,
    I might return renewed.
But where shall I go this summer?

Sweet Jennie's still at Grossinger's;
    St. Andrew's by-the-Sea;
A windjammer wants passengers
    Of whom one *could* be me.
Oh, where shall I go this summer?

Where shall I go this summer? Oh,
    Where shall I spend July?
Kamp Kinder Kute, Camp Bide-a-Wee?
    The sands of Jones or Rye?

With half of every Saturday
    And all of Sunday off,
I'll keep a gin-and-tonic by
    My deck chair on the roof.
That's where I'll be this summer. Oh,
    That's where I'll be this summer.

Debarking First Class, Cabin, Tourist,
   The roaring innocents come home,
Whose motives still are of the purest,
   Whose Yankee dollars are in Rome.

The world's white hope and blackest menace,
   Redolent with Chanel Cinq,
They bear their leather goods from Venice
   Lightly down the long gangplank.

Hollywood's changing British speech,
   They'll tell you, Paris is all chrome,
The Lido's rather like Jones Beach,
   In Leicester Square you think you're home.

If London's a little on the outs,
   It's brave, of that they're certain;
You can even get used to Brussels sprouts
   And a seven-thirty curtain.

They've sat in St.-Germain with Sartre
   And a swell couple from Cheyenne;
"It's a small world," they've said in Chartres,
   In Pisa, then in Aix-les-Bains.

[160]

Dismissing what once seemed banal
  In Michigan and Utah,
They've floated down the Grand Canal
  Con pasta e con frutta.

They've dined on octopi and snails,
  Lived for weeks on *vin rosé;*
From Harry's Bar they've seen red sails
  Drag homeward at the end of day.

About the arts, *anciens, nouveaux,*
  Their judgments are informed and ready;
In France they've seen *les caves de Lascaux,*
  In England, "My Fair Lady."

"Yankee — Go Home," they've read in France,
  "Il Duce!" on a Tuscan wall;
"Visitez l'URSS — Pour Vos Vacances" —
  That Gallic humor over all.

In Florence they've apprized the cost
  Of war in shell and mortar;
The Ponte Vecchio they've crossed
  With Dante and Cole Porter.

They know the price of vice in Naples,
  They've seen the Duke with *her* in Cannes;
The proof is on their baggage labels:
  Travel maketh a full man.

CAPE ANN: A VIEW

TROPIC of ice —
the sea a razor-line toward Spain.
This house I rented on the first of June
already hums with bees about their pueblos,
and from a bare deck rotted by the sun
I see bird islands and the snow-patched slopes
where sea gulls hold their raucous councils.
In single file,
as if they had pried apart the whaleback rock
that shoulders my front door, late irises
shuck off their thin rag-paper wrappings
and stand like roosters while their petals blow.

Again the fond summer comes to a grim edge
off which, this morning, one gray lobsterman
goes trolleying from float to float
and stops at each, his bubbling motorboat
adrift, to rake the sea.
Becalmed, he hauls a shower to his knees,
measures his catch in ounces and in inches,
and, patient, throws out almost everything.
He swings about,
steadfast, his motor muttering, as if with hope,
and fades like a dead soul, still standing up.

A rusty lilac knocks against a shingle;
the old GE refrigerator champs and snores.
When echoes echo in too many rooms,

I go downstairs, compelled to open doors
as if someone stood waiting there . . .
Cold sun steps in. There's little to surprise
a stranger in this neighborhood.

Whoever lives here must be gone for good;
his lavish water colors bleed and sag,
his breadbox is unhinged, his tacked-up wall map
of the zodiac's washed brown with rain;
his pantry shelf keeps one white plate — on it
someone once painted a high-buttoned shoe;
upstairs, there's a wan piece of art nouveau
and a black sweater gone in the right sleeve.

My relics, fallen among his,
lean on the shelves of a long afternoon.
A trapezoid of light goes crabwise on the floor,
the bees with Yo-yo spoolings lift and sink
on the still air, and, in a thrust of gold,
a spider's little partly finished net
abstracts the heart of treachery.

The evening, at first screened in clear pastels,
soon washes out in a romantic clamor.
Gulls on a fishhouse roof,
spaced perfectly, a wing apart, observe
these last annunciations of the visible.
The stars come thick; and as I move
toward sleep within the sleep of walls
that may recall my tenancy, fish, lion,
scorpion and ram climb the important track
from whose solicitous and shining grace
a name descends on the anonymous.

AMERICAN PLAN

THE antique Indian should be Henry James,
  Notebook in hand, a well-disguised impostor;
The porch should (spiritually) face the Thames
  And not the Vineyard or East Gloucester.

The jukebox in the Palm Court should play Herbert
  For ladies quite exhausted from croquet;
The chocolate Popsicle should be lime sherbet
  Served in a glass on a hand-painted tray.

The man in the Hawaiian wrap-around
  Should wear white flannels and a State Street boater;
His wife on water skis across the Sound
  Should make her bread-and-butter calls by motor.

His daughter in the slacks should loll and dally
  Under a parasol from Maison Worth;
The things her madcap girl-chums say should really
  Put her in stitches, into gales of mirth.

The Chris-Craft should be an Old Town Canoe;
  The yellow Jeepster in the porte-cochere
Should be a Willys-Overland tonneau,
  Equipped with robes, ferns, curtains and a spare.

When rats desert a bather's hair-do, all
  Well-meaning sympathy should quite unnerve her;
To thwart the masher and the ne'er-do-well,
  The bathing dress should be a life preserver.

Photographers with tripod, hood and birdie,
  Should take group portraits on the tennis lawn;
The families should look joyless, drawn, but sturdy:
  Men standing, women seated, children prone.

From cupola and minaret should fly
  The flags of summertime, good, old and windswept.
("Gay Whirl at Ocean House," reported by
  The *New York Herald* and the *Boston Transcript.*)

For jolly times that should be had by all,
  For moonlight sings, for roundelay and ballad,
The picnic launch should leave the boathouse full
      Of citronella and potato salad.

The Kodachrome should be a freehand drawing
  (The bathing beach seen from the bathhouse door)
Showing the sunset on the long withdrawing
  Tide and, dimly, figures on the shore.

THE OAK ROOM: AN ELEGY

ACQUAINTED with this world for eighty springs,
Its mortal enemy for more than twenty,
The grandly ancient count the cost of things
And shrink with hunger in the horn of plenty.

In leathern clubrooms, nodding on the *Journal*,
The vested on their watch chains tell the days;
The bent ex-president chats with the colonel
And never hears a word of what he says.

Strange, how their early years come picture-clear,
The time between grown cloudy with conjecture:
In 1912 — was it some other year? —
Old Samuel Clemens gave his final lecture.

Money was money then, a right divine
Embossed on sheets, engraved on silver plates,
As the screaming eagle sang "Sweet Adeline"
Across the length of forty-seven states.

On liners creaking with rich woods and silk,
Their food on swords came flaming to the table;
In the Grand Saloons that held them and their ilk
Alaskan seal played loo with Russian sable.

Among the whiskered, whaleboned and well-rumped —
Unter den Linden, Alexanderplatz —
Der Kaiser Kommt! they called, *Der Kaiser Kommt!*
And doffed fedoras and bowed their ostrich hats.

Their home-grown saints were Vanderbilts and Astors,
Their sweet-voiced angel, Minnie Maddern Fiske;
They weighed the groaning board at Tony Pastor's
With Oysters Rockefeller, lobster bisque,

And wept in Mumms to think where Mory dwells.
If the time was late that seemed so morning-early,
Their strength was sorely taxed, but nothing else,
And the gates of their Tuxedo Park were pearly.

When darling Nellie Melba was the toast
Of capitals around the seven seas,
The ball was all but over; still the host
Waltzed in the arms of his securities.

If their last wills spell out particulars
Almost as out of style as out of reach,
Dull in the railyard sun, their private cars
Rot in the weedy shuntings at Palm Beach.

Mark them. You'll fare no better, spoil no less.
And when their hands, clenched finally, refuse
To take your antiseptic palms in theirs,
Bless them. They had another world to lose.

And when they rail and mumble at the turn
Of things such power and such glory forced,

Permit them their indignity; they burn
In witness that the worse comes to the worst.

Bewildered strangers in the world they made,
Their eyes are grave, their blue lips thinly set:
Lord God of hosts — the imperial echoes fade —
Lest we forget, Lord God, lest we forget.

VERMONT: 7 P.M.

OVER the druid distance, mountains and mist:
Vermont calls home her handsome cattle, looks
For further weather on the paralleling slopes.

At the lookout point, alone, a tourist stops
Cold to the bone, while mountains like breakers roll
Forest on shuddering forest toward his eyes.

In the scriptured towns, graveyard seniority
(Republican up to the stone-cut brows)
Assures a future in the sprawling daisies,

While each undaunted face that walks the street
Winters in history. Where cubist pines
Lean on the rocky waters, cabins keep

Poets and painters and their casual sex
Of summer in the so-called temperate zone;
Where the female college stands on the fabled run

That bloodies out the history text with war,
Potato pickers learn the dancer's weird
Sophistication, and the poet's witless eyes.

Yet the millstone native growls to hear
His life in easy epic so translated,
As though Vermont were that America,

The Stars and Stripes become a drop scene for
Ballets and eclogues. And if they are right,
If homespun anger is a clue to truth,

Nobody knows or cares. The culture of
The urban wintertime, its dancing boys,
Its lottery of lights, will show Vermont

As that unique geography no pen
Controls, no bar of sound domesticates.
The old green Yankee apple's bitter with

Headstones, winter and cracked promises;
No alien knows what must, hard-knuckled, hold
Its desperate emptiness, its years to come.

CARMARTHEN BAR

Hung between stretched wings, the sea bird sat —
A shape of pain — not far from where we walked
In heavy light from off Carmarthen Bar.
"Mad Christ," I said, "Christ of the cormorants,"
But you interpreted him differently —
"He thinks that's what a cormorant *should* do,
Nobody ever told him otherwise."
All morning and all afternoon, we ached
To see his Satan-pointed shoulders make
A shrinking crucifix on the wet sand.

Perhaps, had we had more to do than climb
Sir John's Hill for the seaward view, or read
Half-finished verses in the summerhouse,
We should have heard his limp cry less, or less
Insistently. But, as it was, with words
Falling and rain falling and a drum
Nobody heard, the bird's predicament —
Was he a god in whose reach, uttermost
And pitiable, only himself was caught? —
Embroiled us when we had least heart for it.

That night within Laugharne Castle when the moon's
Seagoing trumpet blew out half the stars,
And field mice whimpered, and a chuckling owl
Cartwheeled above us in the roofless light,
The human darkness of eight hundred years
Bled from a cry. It was the cormorant.
As if, by speech, we might still overtake
A mystery we could not escape, I said,
"Sweet Christus of the cormorants outstretched,"
And you said, "Bloody bird," and nudged me home.

By morning our old albatross was gone.
Did the tides take him, sprawled on his black rack?
Or was he mustered upward, his dead wings
Beating toward immolation ceaselessly?
The angel in him, or the idiot,
Had driven us away. Yet when I cried,
"Christ Cormorant, that you might scavenge me!"
Without reflection you looked down to find
His black cross posted in that shining sand.
Together then we smiled, and walked inland.

"THE terrible girls have outlived all that silver,"
Said the matron from St. Louis, Mo.,
And the taxi down from Reno every night
Waits by the prefab cottage door
Under the one red light.

"How strange that in this mountain rock the graves
Are marked with wood," said the clerk from Cleveland, O.,
And the worms get through another wind-smooth cross,
And the playbill face of Joseph Jefferson
Peels from the Opera House.

"Buy me a drink where Mark Twain wrote that book,"
Said the blonde from Pasadena, Cal.,
And where the streets fall off into clear sky
The Indian in the G.I. shoes
Watches the Fords go by.

"Look, genuine nuggets from the Comstock Lode,"
Said the dentist from Port Huron, Mich.,
And minerals glitter in his thinning blood
Where death made a killing in the hills
And settled down for good.

"Ten silver dollars for the slot machine,"
Said the bride from Providence, R.I.,
And where the hurricanes of avarice
Once passed, the jukebox in the Last Chance Bar
Opens its silver voice.

[173]

NIGHT of a sudden walks out of the sea;
  A zephyr from Grand Cayman sighs;
The Governor's lady pours high tea;
  Mama spoons up her peas and rice.

A carriage lamp is lighted, and at last
  The market women shroud their stalls;
The coral islands, fortunate and blessed,
  Sing like wind-fumbled shells

As hummingbird and curled-up scorpion
  Cling lightly to blood-purple flowers
And in the warm footprint of the sun
  Limelight climbs the pirate's tower.

One palm tree, like a rotted windmill, creaks;
  The night grows insect-deep and balmy;
Though screens and peeling shutters leaks
  Calypso music from Miami.

Perfumed by bougainvillaea and rum,
  The dollar-laden trade winds blow
As the shakers shake and the wires hum
  For Dirty Dick and Sloppy Joe.

Rain-pocked, perhaps amused, Victoria
    Wipes moonlight from her granite knees;
"*Sic transit gloria,*"
    She says, "from Whitehall to the Caribbees."

On the childish face of the post-office clock,
    Time burns; the dawn winds sough and sway;
A crab scuds from a dripping rock;
    The Dog Star swims away

As the late moon, afloat on a blue reef,
    Silvers the gatherers of shells,
And the world's conspicuously rich sleep safe
    In their big peppermint hotels.

"ICH AM OF IRLAUNDE"

WHERE sea gulls, holy-ghosting rainbows, ran
With the weather on the piebald landfall lea,
I came to Ireland, an Irishman,
To dress a grave for *saynte charité*;
Since I could bare no emblem, stag or swan,
And stood three generations out of fee,
I held my tongue, and crossed my knife and fork
In the black kitchens of the County Cork.

Morning that breaks a prodigal to sight
Brought squires, bitch-hard ladies, fat priests who,
Gifted with gab, grace, and good appetite,
Bellwethered ignorance into its pew;
While under high Heaven and the low birth rate
Potato pickers fed the status quo,
Barbaric stallions, hitched to brass-hung drays,
Rolled thunder from imperial breweries.

On the cross of the Celt I laid my wreath.
My father's hand in mine kept my heart still:
Once more, under a Yankee shibboleth,
We walked the slattern side of Beacon Hill
On the seventeenth of March. To prove our faith,
A crosier pointed and the State House fell;
The lace-curtain banners of the Boston poor
Hoisted the tribe of Brennan-on-the-Moor.

Full summer in their suit, sheep-soft with corn,
The lowing meadows of my race and creed
Beguiled my rite, as if a far-off horn,
Lifting to summons neither quick nor dead,
Sang the long daydreams of cromlech and cairn
And would with bees and heather fill my head.
To the invitations of that afternoon
I had come late; blood would not flow from stone.

Twilight on castle keep and highland throne
Brought Sean from his alehouse, Deirdre from her shop.
Their sorrows had a name; their day was done.
If from a blazing vault some druid shape
Keened on cold cottage and pinchpenny town,
Who was my witness? All night, fast asleep,
Toward Dublin in the rocking Night Mail curled,
I wept for visions, nothing in the world.

HOTEL PARADISO E COMMERCIALE

ANOTHER hill town:
another dry Cinzano in the sun.
I couldn't sleep in that enormous echo —
silence and water music, sickly street lamps
neither on nor off — a night
of islands and forgotten languages.

Yet morning, marvellously frank, comes up
with bells, with loaves, with letters
distributed like gifts. I watch a fat priest
spouting grape seeds, a family weeping
in the fumes of a departing bus.

This place is nowhere
except on the map. Wheels spin the sun,
with a white clatter shutters are shut to,
umbrellas bloom in striped and sudden groves.
The day's away, impossibly the same,
and only minutes are at all important —
if women by a wall,
a lean dog, and a cheerful humpback
selling gum and ball-points
are important. My glass is empty.
It is Wednesday. It is not going to rain.

Observation
without speculation. How soon
the eye craves what it cannot see,
goes limpid, glazed, unanswerable,
lights on a pigeon walking in a circle,
hangs on a random shadow,
would rather sleep.

How old am I?
What's missing here? What do these people
feed on, that won't feed on them? This town
needs scrolls, celestial delegations,
a swoon of virgins, apostles in apple green,
a landscape riding on a holy shoulder.

The morning stays.
As though I kept an old appointment,
I start by the cats' corridors (Banco di Roma,
wineshops, gorgeous butcheries)
toward some mild angel of annunciation —
upstairs, most likely, badly lit,
speaking in rivets on a band of gold.

Praise God, this town keeps one
unheard-of masterpiece to justify
a million ordinary mornings
and pardon this one.

FLIGHT 539

Tʜᴇ same March sun that polishes St. Paul's
brightens the arches of my rack of toast.
I am flying, after breakfast, to North America.
I crack my egg with an egg-spoon; it is almost

time. I yank at straps, count money and check out,
saluted by a doorman with a calfskin face
who carries one fawn glove and wears the other.
I'm glum but genial; he's aloof. He knows his place

and clearly indicates I should know mine.
London that shone at my descent with brass
militia, geraniums, throngs of happy subjects
acting naturally, now lets me pass

as though I'd packed up and left yesterday.
"Never hinder a traveler," it says, "never detain
a guest." Its thin smile reaches to the airport.
I am not happy until I see my plane,

grasshopper-still, in fog that crowds like sleep
outside the waiting room. There is "a slight delay."
I buy five-fifths of White Horse and a Penguin
Classic that I should have read and, squared away,

slump in a wicker chair. Nothing happens
for hours. I watch a covey of white nuns who gaily
chirp toward their oblivion in Africa,
a delegation handing roses to a swart Israeli

who weeps and smiles, important in blue serge.
Do they know, I wonder, just where they belong?
My passport photo, smirking, looks me in the eye.
Loudspeakers call my number: I must go along

with all my flight companions to Gate 9.
Two by two, bellwethered by a china doll,
we file out, mount the ramp, take one last look around,
and find our seats to music piped through a wall

of leatherette. We have all done this before; we're bored
and terrified. Full tilt, our backbones braced
by gravity, we run wide open, lift,
punch through a wadding cloud and, clear at last,

track a bent circle over dunes and troughs,
riding a blue ecliptic toward the Hebrides.
The monitory lights go off, we drop our belts
and sit, heads back, alike as effigies.

Five hours that I fattened on in coming over
drop off at once. I know the time, but what time is it?
I light a cigarette off Scotland and crush the butt
some eighty miles at sea. The pilot says it

's cold in Boston, that turbulence off Newfoundland
won't reach us since we're six miles up and will soon
go up to seven. I scan the dome of the known world,
trying to imagine what I see. I'd like someone

to talk to. So would the man behind me.
We stand, stretch out, yawning like old familiars,
unembarrassed, going home. He's been
in Asia Minor where, he says, "our" failures

are conspicuous. Pleased to worry this old bone,
we share our guilt like men of the same kidney.
Then, bumped apart, we sink through clouds which,
we are told almost at once, are over Sydney,

Nova Scotia. We shake hands and, separately, sit down,
having just parted forever. The coast line filters through —
a ragged lace of ice on the North Shore. Then it's
Nahant, Revere Beach smudged with drifts of snow

that look left over from an age of ice.
Leveling, we come down fast and, drifting slightly
(a gull goes by like wreckage from a blast)
in a fan of sun, are thumped to earth as lightly

as an apple from a bough. Is it still two o'clock?
I'm stretched among northern lights! I'm lost on
a reef surrounded by dim bubbles! "Ladies and gentlemen,"
the stewardess says, "we have landed in Boston."